KT-116-721

REAL ITALIAN FOOD

REAL ITALIAN FOOD

THE REGIONAL RECIPES OF ITALY'S CUCINA TIPICA

Paul Lay

CONRAN OCTOPUS

First published in 2004 by
Conran Octopus Limited, a part of
the Octopus Publishing Group
2–4 Heron Quays
London E14 4JP

To order please ring Conran Octopus Direct
on 01903 828503

Volume copyright © 2004 by Breslich & Foss Ltd
Location photography © 2004 by Anna Watson
Text by Paul Lay
Recipe photography by Phil Wilkins
Home economy and styling by Mandy Phipps
Designed by Elizabeth Healey
Cartography by Julian Baker
Index by Peter Barber

Paul Lay has asserted his moral right to be identified
as author of this work in accordance with the
Copyright, Designs and Patents Act, 1988.

All rights reserved. No part of this publication may
be reproduced or transmitted in any form or by any
means, electronic or mechanical, including
photocopying, recording or by any information
storage-and-retrieval system, without prior written
permission from the publisher.

A catalogue record for this book is available from the
British Library.

ISBN 1 84091 373 8

Conceived and produced by
Breslich & Foss Ltd
Unit 2A, Union Court
20–22 Union Road
London SW4 6JP

Printed in China

CONTENTS

INTRODUCTION

Italians are rarely seduced by the pursuit of novelty. Western Europe's most conservative country sticks to what it knows best, especially when it comes to its great passions: food and football. Even in its great cities, few restaurants serve the cuisines of other cultures; not many serve even the dishes of other Italian regions. In Rome, or Milan there will be the odd, usually very bad Chinese restaurant or, more reliably, an Ethiopian or Eritrean eaterie, reminders of ill-fated ventures in East Africa perpetrated by Mussolini's Fascists. But one is no more likely to happen upon foreign food in Italy than to witness an Italian football match characterised by attacking flair. It's just not the done thing. For all the talk of Latin passion and romance, Italians are marked by their caution.

This is not to say that Italians are unwelcoming to the outsider. Italian society has a cultural certainty that allows for little self-doubt so, ironically, anyone who, like me, seeks to understand its gastronomic glories is almost smothered by the welcome, such is the understandable pride of a people in the country's remarkable cultural legacy, and especially its world-conquering cuisine.

The idea for this book – to visit the places where the country's most famous dishes were born, and to sample them at their most authentic – first came to me in probably the greatest, certainly the most relentlessly 'Italian' of all the

Opposite: Pasta and wild herb pesto are dished up at the Maionchi family's Tuscan retreat.

Above: Wonderful food markets abound in Italy; a drum of matured Parmesan cheese.

country's great cities: Naples. I was astonished to discover that its tight, baroque alleys were home to scores of spit-and-sawdust pizzerias producing a dish of which the versions sold elsewhere in the world were pale imitations. My first taste of a Neapolitan pizza marinara, eaten on the bare marble tables of the Antica Pizzeria Da Michele, was an epiphanal moment. At once I understood the virtues of Italian food: fresh ingredients, cooked with the minimum of fuss. In the 20 years since that encounter, the Italian diet – rich in vegetables, fruit and complex carbohydrates, washed down, of course, by a little (and it is always a little) wine – has become the benchmark of healthy eating.

Travelling from the Alpine North to Sicily, I have been lucky to encounter not only real Italian food, but also some remarkable people, all of them committed to the maintenance of traditional culinary excellence. Some, like those at Turin's Lavazza coffee company or the cheese and ham makers of Parma, belong to large outfits that sell their products around the world; most, like the pasta-makers of Bologna, or the bakers of Puglia, are part of modest, patient operations, serving a loyal local market with the odd foray further; a few – the sweet makers of Sicily, or the restaurateurs of Venice with their divine offerings of risotto – are just individuals offering products made anew by hand every day and sold only on their own premises. All make a good living. And at a time of great pessimism, when so many fret about the disappearance of small producers, Italy bucks the trend. Those who have stuck to the traditional methods of production – and combine it with a little marketing know-how – are selling their products not only to a vigorous domestic market, but one that reaches much further afield, to the rest of Europe, North America and beyond.

Above: A butcher's counter in Bologna, home of ragù.

Below: A little oil tops the classic Neapolitan pizza.

This book is not meant to be – it could not be – definitive. Each chapter is a snapshot, of talented, conscientious people achieving excellence in their chosen field. Nor is it a book for the cook seeking innovation and novelty. I have sought out those dishes that reflect the deepest traditions of Italian cuisine. Most are simple and quick; the more difficult simply require a little more time and care to prepare. All will serve four people well. Of course, none will quite recreate the magic of eating such classics in the confines of a Neapolitan pizzeria, or a Venetian osteria while lingering over a glass of wine. There is no substitute for that. But I hope they do give you a taste for real Italian food.

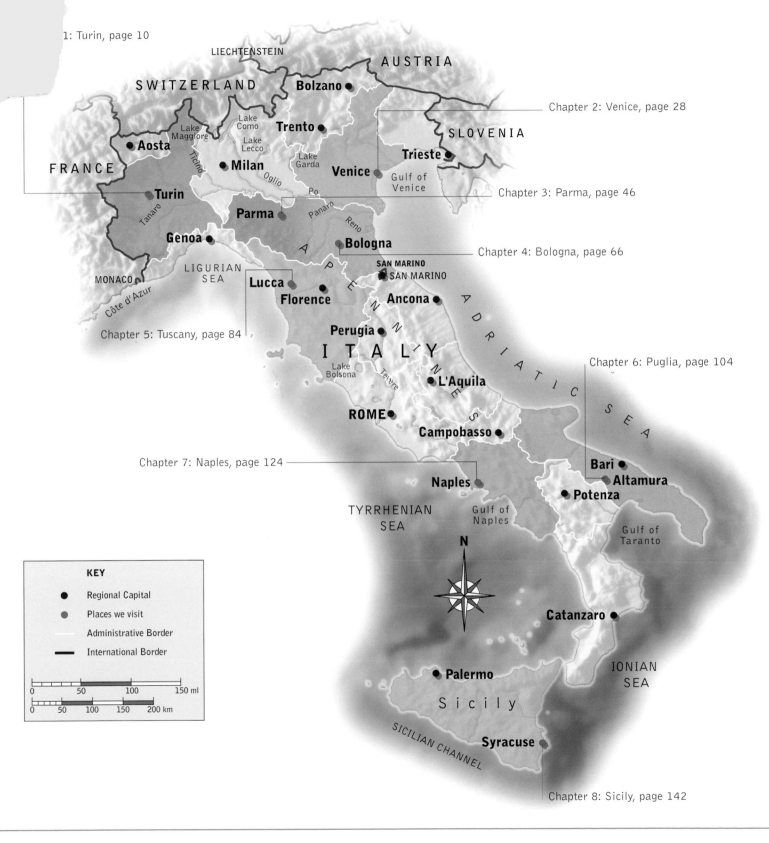

1: Turin, page 10

LIECHTENSTEIN

AUSTRIA

SWITZERLAND

Bolzano ●

Lake
Como

Trento ●

Chapter 2: Venice, page 28

Lake
Maggiore

SLOVENIA

Aosta ●

Lake
Lecco

Lake
Garda

Trieste ●

FRANCE

Ticino

Milan ●

Venice ●

Oglio

Gulf of
Venice

Turin ●

Po

Tanaro

Parma ●

Panaro

Reno

Chapter 3: Parma, page 46

Genoa ●

A
P
E
N
N
I
N
E
S

Bologna ●

Chapter 4: Bologna, page 66

LIGURIAN
SEA

SAN MARINO
● SAN MARINO

MONACO

Lucca ●

A
D
R
I
A
T
I
C

Côte d'Azur

Florence ●

Ancona ●

Chapter 5: Tuscany, page 84

Perugia ●

I T A L Y

Lake
Bolsona

Chapter 6: Puglia, page 104

S
E
A

Tevere

L'Aquila ●

ROME ●

Campobasso ●

Bari ●

Chapter 7: Naples, page 124

Altamura

Naples ●

Potenza ●

TYRRHENIAN
SEA

Gulf of
Naples

Gulf of
Taranto

N

IONIAN
SEA

Catanzaro ●

KEY

● Regional Capital

● Places we visit

Administrative Border

International Border

Palermo ●

0   50   100   150 ml

S i c i l y

0   50   100   150   200 km

SICILIAN CHANNEL

Syracuse ●

Chapter 8: Sicily, page 142

CHAPTER 1: TURIN

CAFE SOCIETY

It may come as a surprise to some, but the Italians don't actually drink that much coffee. They come way down a European league of consumption headed by caffeine-happy Scandinavians. The dominance of the espresso in Italian cafe society, that small thimbleful of concentrated taste and aroma, ensures the intake remains relatively low; the very nature of Italian coffee-making is designed to get a great deal from very little.

THE BREAKFAST RITUAL

Even in the most deprived and isolated rural backwaters of Italy, there will be a bar with an expensive Gaggia machine, ready to deliver the beverages on which Italy seems to run. The ritual breakfast of cappuccino – one part espresso to three parts milk – and cornetto, the more substantial Italian take on the croissant, grabbed at the bar and eaten on the go, is ubiquitous throughout the peninsula. Around 10.30am, the espresso takes over, taken at regular intervals to percolate the day. When Italians ask for 'un caffè', an espresso is what they get.

Of all cups of coffee drunk by the average Italian each week, two-thirds will be espresso, knocked back, promptly,

unadulterated. According to one Italian purist: 'black coffee doesn't need sugar: an average one needs sugar, and a bad one needs help with milk.'

The Italian experience at its most basic is an everyday artform taken for granted by the millions who partake of it. But in the northern Italian city of Turin, coffee is never taken for granted. Here, the pursuit of the bean reaches unparalleled heights of quality and sophistication. Its cafes are a mecca for the connoisseur.

The icons of Turin, capital of the province of Piedmont, are those of modern Italy. This stately, compact city in the shade of the Alps is home to FIAT, the Agnelli family's industrial powerhouse, which churns out the little Fiat Puntos that clog the cramped streets of the country's

Opposite : Archetypal symbols of Turin: enjoying the newspaper, a coffee, and a cigarette; the interior of Caffè Torino; the ubiquitous Fiat cinquecento.

Above : A traditionally attired waiter at Lavazza's cafe, San Tommaso 10, serves 'solid coffee', an elaborate northern take on traditional granità.

'The lighter roast is preferred in the North, there's less caffeine, and it's better balanced. Yes, they like their coffee bitter in the South. And then they put a great big dollop of sugar in it. It's madness.'

André Fucci

Above: One of Lavazza's collection of antique coffee-making machines.

historic centres, and crafts the Ferraris and Alfa Romeos that exemplify the genius of Italian engineering and design. Juventus, *la signora vecchia*, the grand old lady of Italian football, resides in Turin's Stadio delle Alpe. Another of the Agnelli's crown jewels – 'Juve' as it is known to its fans – is the best-supported, arguably the most successful and certainly the most envied of the elite clubs of Serie A, Italy's first division. Olivetti, the computer manufacturer, its output visible in every Italian bank, post office and supermarket, is yet another of Turin's triumphs.

FIRST CAPITAL OF ITALY

These commercial successes reflect the purposeful, disciplined nature of Turin. It is, at first glance, the least Italian, certainly the least Mediterranean of all the nation's great regional capitals. When one walks through its elegant grid of porticoed galleries and wide avenues, Paris and Vienna come to mind, and it shares with those cities an abundance of art deco cafes, centred on Piazza San Carlo, Turin's 'living room'.

Yet no city did more to forge the identity of modern Italy. At the centre of Piazza San Carlo, very much a symbol of the city, stands the equestrian statue of Emanuele Filiberto, his great sword thrust downwards; Filiberto, Duke of Savoy, won independence from France and Spain at the battle of San Quinitino in 1574, unifying Piedmont. Almost three centuries later, his descendant, Carlo Emanuele III, forged an unlikely alliance with his liberal prime minister Camillo Cavour and the southern revolutionary Giuseppe Garibaldi, to make Turin the driving force of the *Risorgimento*, the movement to unite Italy's disparate regions and bring to an end centuries of foreign dominance.

Within a decade the country was one, at least in name, and Carlo's son, Vittorio Emanuele, was crowned King of Italy in 1870. For a short while Turin was the new nation's capital. When Rome swiftly took up the mantle, Turin was reduced to the capital of the predominantly rural province of Piedmont, but found its deliverance in industry. Turin's new-found affluence fuelled a sophisticated urban lifestyle with the cafe at its core.

Connoisseurs argue endlessly over the question, which is the finest cafe in Turin? There's no doubting the oldest. The Caffè Confetteria al Bicerin on Piazza della Consolata dates from 1763, and takes its name from its speciality: a bicerin.

Making the perfect *cappuccino*.

1. A finely powdered espresso blend is packed into the strainer.

2. An espresso is freshly made.

3. Milk is heated by steam bursting through the machine's narrow spigot, creating a dense froth.

4. Milk is added to an espresso at the ratio of three to one, creating *cappuccino*, the drink being the same colour as the habits worn by Capuchin monks.

Torta di nocciola

Hazelnut cake

Piedmont is Italy's most traditional wine-producing region, and probably its best. Expensive and rich, the wine called Barolo, made from the Nebbiolo grape is produced near the city of Alba, south-east of Turin. But the vine is not the only fruit of Alba's sloping, sub-Alpine terraces. The region's hazelnuts are of the highest quality, and though eaten freshly shelled they are unbeatable, especially in winter, this coarse, rustic cake embodies the simple, sweet pleasures of Piedmont's mountain country.

Ingredients

200g (7oz) peeled hazelnuts

3 medium eggs, separated

1 tablespoon baking powder

100g (3oz) sugar

100g (3oz) unsalted butter

200g (7oz) plain flour

grated rind of 1 lemon

125ml (4fl oz) milk

1. Toast the hazelnuts under a medium grill for 5 minutes, checking frequently to make sure they don't burn.
2. Chop the nuts coarsely in a blender or food processor.

Right: A board advertises the rich mixture of coffee, dark chocolate and cream called a bicerin, in honour of the famous cafe.

Opposite: The Caffé Confetteria al Bicerin was founded in 1763. It was a favourite of Italy's first prime minister, Emilio Cavour.

'Bicerin', in the local dialect, translates as 'something delicious', and one can only agree. It's a luscious drink of coffee, chocolate and a dab of cream, often accompanied, by a bagnato, a moist mouthful of biscuit.

A GROUND-BREAKING CAFE

In its time, Al Bicerin was a groundbreaker. Owned by women, it was frequented by them too, against the traditions of the time. Later, Cavour, the agnostic, whiled away his time there on Sunday mornings as his royal allies took communion in the adjacent Santuario della Consolata. The philosopher Nietzsche, who adored Turin – 'it is a city after my own heart' – was an habitué too, as was the Tuscan composer Puccini who, it is said, introduced a scene into his opera *Manon Lescaut* after seeing prisoners paraded outside the cafe's windows. The same high

3. Beat the egg yolks and baking powder together thoroughly until smooth.

4. Add all the remaining ingredients except the egg whites and mix thoroughly.

5. Beat the egg whites until they are stiff, then fold them into the mixture gently by hand.

6. Pour the cake mixture into a buttered 20cm (8in) diameter cake tin, and bake at 200°C (400°F) gas mark 6 for 30 minutes or until brown. Serve while still warm.

standards of window dressing are maintained to this day. The displays are mirrored inside, with torte, gelati and zabaglione tempting customers to the cabinets that stand below a stupendous marble bar.

The turn of the century saw a spate of stylish cafes being built that survive to this day. The Caffè Torino is a classic, its carved wooden ceiling and heavy floral decoration a dramatic backdrop to its colourful displays of pastries and chocolates. Located at the city's heart, it is calm, quiet, orderly, noted for its impeccable service, and almost unchanged since its opening in 1903. Turnaround inside is fast, espressos are downed quickly at the imposing bar, in keeping with Turin's feel of studious efficiency. A chocolate might be taken as accompaniment. Turin, after all, is the city where chocolate as we know it was first made.

CHOCOLATE HEAVEN

The tradition is maintained at Peyrano, a chocolate manufacturer founded in 1915 by Giacomo Peyrano, a champion rower. It's presently in the hands of the third generation of the same family, and sited on the opposite bank of the Po. Giuseppe Peyrano, who began working here in 1953, and his son Antonio run the workshop surrounded by the machinery of the traditional chocolatier: a roaster, a cocoa-crusher, a refiner, a mortar to mix the cocoa and sugar, and, more recently, a *melangeur*, or mixer. The remarkable management skills of Bruna Peyrano, wife of Giacomo's brother, Giorgio, ensure that the company holds its unbeaten position as the best chocolatier in town and supplier to the best cafes, including the Caffè Torino.

Outside the Caffè Torino, beneath vast porticoes on which hangs a neon Martini sign (a reminder of Vermouth's Torinese origins), ladies who lunch predominate, tucking into more Peyrano specialities such as almond-flavoured gianduiotti, as well as torta de nocciola and torta de cioccolata, the leads of their little dogs lashed to padded chairs. The delicately made, beautifully presented chocolate typical of Peyrano's output, is an adult pleasure. The Italians are no more gluttons of chocolate than they are gluttons of coffee. Quality is all.

On Piazza Castello, near to where the reunified Italy's first parliament convened, is the small Caffè Mulassano, a near-contemporary of Caffè Torino, built in 1907 by Antonio Vandone, and its equal in beauty. Though essentially art deco, it has a touch of the baroque about it, not least because of the elaborate wall carvings and the imposing, jangling and very old cash register that stands on the bar. Even a glass of water is an experience here, served through two spigots, that quietly hiss above the hum of chatter. Mulassano lays claim to the invention, in 1925, of the tramezzini, the elaborate triple-deckered Italian sandwich that is now found nationwide.

Above, top: Giuseppe Peyrano stands before some finely crafted chocolates. The company was founded in 1915.

Above: The antique cash register of Caffè Mulassano is still in noisy, everyday use.

Opposite: The dining room of the Caffè Torino, salon of Turin's elite.

Espresso

Espresso

It is impossible to recreate the Torinese (or, indeed, the Italian) espresso without investing in a professional quality machine. But, do as the Italians do and buy a good domestic *moka* – Bialetti are among the best makes – and you'll get a very good approximation. Success depends on the blend of coffee used, and the amount. Do not skimp. Fill the chamber of the *moka* to the brim: the coffee must have a kick. As for blends, Lavazza (especially their crema e gusto blend) and Illy (from the Adriatic port of Trieste) are now widely available in northern Europe and America, and Italian delicatessens will sell a wider range still. If in Italy, look out for the more bitter southern blends such as Kiko, or the superb Roman blend, Castroni. Surprisingly, many of the best Italian coffees are made not from the prized Arabica bean but from the Robusta bean, which is underrated and neglected elsewhere.

To make 4 small cups (tazzine) of espresso coffee:

1. Fill the bottom compartment of a 400ml (14 fl oz) *moka* three-quarters full with fresh, cold water.
2. Pack the filter with your choice of espresso blend, and screw on the *moka* top.
3. Place on the hob over a medium heat and, as soon as the water begins to boil remove from the heat (boiled coffee is bad coffee).
4. Allow the coffee to filter through to the top, then pour immediately into tazzine. Serve with or without sugar.

Here are three ways to adapt an espresso. Stir the milk as it is slowly brought to the boil:

macchiato

To make this very popular 'stained' coffee, add only 1 or 2 teaspoons of boiled milk to an espresso.

cappuccino

This is traditionally served with breakfast and takes 3 parts boiled milk to 1 of coffee. Use an *aerolatte* to froth the hot milk, then pour slowly into the coffee.

latte

Make this milky coffee by adding 6 to 8 parts boiled milk to one of coffee.

COFFEE'S DISTANT ORIGINS

Turin didn't invent the espresso or the cappuccino: that honour belongs to Naples, a city with its own contrasting approaches to the beverage. Neither is it Italy's coffee trading centre. Trieste, the old Habsburg port on the Adriatic which links the Latin and Slavic worlds imports most of Italy's raw beans. The coffee plant is not indigenous to Italy or grown there in any significant quantity. Its origins lie in Kaffa, tucked away in the mountains of southern Ethiopia. It spread from there into the Arab world. A cafe is reputed to have opened in Mecca as early as the ninth century. Italy, like the rest of Europe was slow to appreciate the qualities of the 'Arabian wine'.

Venice, with its strong trading links to the Middle East, got there first. Francesco Morosini, Venetian Ambassador to the Ottoman court at Constantinople, reported the presence of Turkish coffee houses, and eventually, in 1615, the first imports of the bean reached the lagoon. The first coffee shop opened in Piazza San Marco in the early 1640s. The coffee-drinking fashion spread quickly throughout western Europe, where coffee became associated with intellectual stimulation. In 1690, Dutch sailors broke the Arab monopoly on the coffee trade when they raided the Red Sea port of Mocha, stole coffee plants and raised them in the Indonesian archipelago. The French did much the same thing, planting areas of the Caribbean, from where the trade spread to South America. Brazil is now the world's number one supplier. But coffee, in the eyes of the world, is *the* Italian drink.

Below left: The art of presentation is highly valued in Italy, as seen in these bags of biscotti in Turin.

Below: Little chocolate fishes are laid out for sale in Turin's cafes.

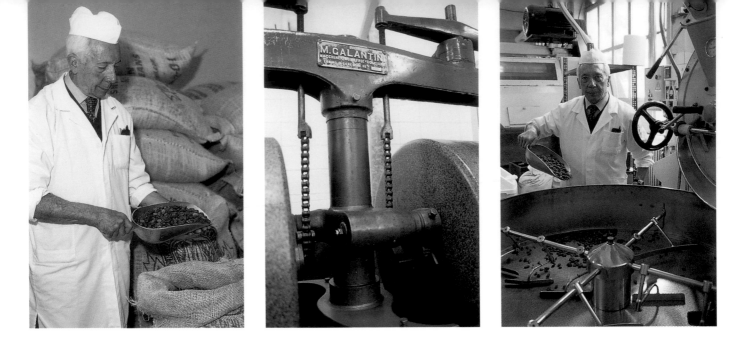

INTENSE AND WONDERFUL

In 1995, to celebrate their centenary, Lavazza, Turin's largest coffee company or *torrefazione*, set about restoring an old grocer's shop and turned it into a smart cafe – San Tommaso 10. It's there that I meet one of Lavazza's experts on everything to do with coffee. Once through the cafe's frosted doors, I share a simple lunch of agnolotti, a delicious filled pasta stuffed with ground pork and cheese, with coffee man, André Fucci. We're surrounded by professionals in the smart casual uniform of Italian business. 'We'll tell you everything you need to know about coffee,' he says. We head for the Lavazza factory in Strada Settimo, a stark, grey, functional building where, inside, green-overalled workers sally back and forth on fork-lift trucks, loading hemp sacks of coffee beans for processing. The smell is intense and wonderful, belying the industrial backdrop.

Coffee in Turin is dominated by Lavazza: 80 per cent of the city's coffee is blended in Strada Settimo. Set up by Luigi Lavazza in 1895, the company remains, in typically Italian fashion, a family concern. Its circular blue logo is found throughout Italy, where it now accounts for almost half the market share. But its success has spread far beyond *il bel paese*. Lavazza products are on the shelves of supermarkets throughout Europe and North America. One no longer needs travel to Italy to get some idea of what coffee should taste like. Lavazza, despite its size and global presence, is a major sponsor of the fast-growing Slow Food Movement, which originated in Piedmont during the 1980s, born it is said in protest at the decision to open a McDonalds near Rome's Spanish Steps. Lavazza is a company that believes big and beautiful can mix, and sets out to prove that profit and quality can co-exist.

Much of Strada Settimo is warehouse, but at its core is a series of pristine workrooms, packed with state-of-the-art espresso machines, the names Gaggia and Faema prominent. Lavazza hold a fine collection of early machines too. The first, the *macchina a vapore*, was produced in Naples at the beginning of the twentieth century, though it was Achille Gaggia, a Milanese engineer, who perfected

Above left:
Giuseppe Peyrano inspects cocoa beans imported from South America and Java.

Above centre:
The beans are ground in Peyrano's traditional grinder.

Above right:
The ground beans are roasted in kilns fired with olive wood before being mixed with sugar and cocoa.

the technique, and whose company now dominates the Italian – and world – market. In the early 1960s, the rival firm of Faema perfected the process, developing a method to heat pressurised cold water rapidly, serving notice on the awkward, bulbous boilers that had been used up till then.

André and I enter the training room, which looks more like a hi-tech research laboratory than a coffee factory. In the centre is a table of metallic sinks into which professional coffee tasters spit out their mouthfuls before passing judgement. The room has the serious air of a draconian courtroom.

A QUESTION OF TASTE

Coffee beans come in two different types: Arabica and Robusta, of which the former is generally considered to be higher in quality. There's a definite North-South divide in Italian coffee tastes. 'The lighter roast is preferred in the North, there's less caffeine, and it's better balanced,' says André. The South prefers strong, full-bodied coffees. 'Yes, they like their coffee bitter in the South,' says André. 'And then they put a great big dollop of sugar in it. It's madness.' At least to his northern Italian tastebuds. André demonstrates the difference: 'This is a tray of Arabica, from Brazil. Like half a peanut. Grey or green in colour.' The Robusta beans he lays before me are smaller, less uniform, in a greater variety of colours.

The process of blending and roasting is unique to each company. The beans are spread out, cleaned and dried, and released into great revolving ovens, like gigantic upturned washing machines, where they are heated to about 220°C (430°F). This is a difficult, measured process. The beans must retain their natural oils while also being brittle enough to smash into the fine powder typical of espresso. Roasting takes about ten minutes. By then the beans are a little lighter in weight and considerably bigger. In this highly mechanised business, it is a computerised program that then selects the appropriate beans for a particular blend.

Above left:
Chocolate in its raw state ready to be moulded.

Above centre:
The finished chocolate is locked away in a cabinet.

Above right:
Peyrano is probably best know for its pralines, but its products come in many shapes.

For the sauce

200ml (7fl oz) extra virgin olive oil

12 tinned anchovies, washed and drained

6 cloves garlic, peeled and minced

1. Gently heat the oil in a small saucepan.
2. Add the anchovies to the oil and stir until they 'melt'.
3. Turn down the heat, add the garlic and stir over a very low heat for 2 or 3 minutes. Do not allow the garlic to brown or burn.
4. Serve in the saucepan.

Bagna cauda
Hot anchovy dip and vegetables

The bagna cauda, or 'hot bath', is perhaps the most distinctive of all Piemontese dishes. Sadly, the favourite vegetable for dipping is the cardoon, a small edible thistle that you won't find on many supermarket shelves outside Italy. A distant relative of the fondue (a reminder of the region's Alpine links), bagna cauda is a simple, typically ingenious creation of peasant culture, and above all a sociable affair. If you can get hold of walnut or hazelnut oils, use those; olive oil is a relatively new addition to Piemontese cuisine. Serve the bagna cauda in the saucepan or in an earthenware dish – the liquid must be kept hot.

For the vegetables

1 carrot, peeled and cut into spears

assorted peppers, sliced

fennel, sliced

broccoli florets

1. Dip the raw vegetables into the hot sauce and eat.

Bollito Misto con Salsa Verde

Slow-cooked meat

If you think boiled meats are dull, try this wonderfully
hearty and tasty dish, the benchmark for northern Italy's
finest restaurants, and a great dish to serve at a large
dinner party; but ensure invitations are restricted to keen
carnivores. Very much the weekend dish of the region, bollito
misto even has its own trolley – the *carrello dei bolliti* –
usually made of silver. Feel free to adapt; the Piemontese
use as many as seven different types of meat in one of their
versions, but the recipe below is the classic.

SERVES 8-10

Ingredients

1 1.5kg (3-3½lb) ox tongue

2 medium carrots, peeled and
   roughly chopped

2 sticks celery, roughly
   chopped

2 medium onions, peeled and
   roughly chopped

1kg (2lb 4oz) silverside of
   beef

1 1.5kg (3-3½lb) chicken

1 precooked Cotechino sausage

1. Place the tongue and the
   vegetables in a large pan
   and cover them with
   boiling water.
2. Bring to the boil, skim the
   surface, and add the beef.
3. Bring to a simmer, cover and
   cook for 1 hour.
4. Add the chicken, bring back
   to a simmer, then cover and
   cook for 2 more hours.
5. Add the sausage and cook
   until heated thoroughly.
6. Skin the tongue and return
   it to the pan.
7. Carve the meats, and serve
   with lightly boiled
   potatoes, carrots, celery
   and salsa verde.

For the salsa verde

225g (8oz) finely chopped
   flat-leaf parsley

30g (1oz) mint, finely chopped

4 tinned anchovies, chopped

1 teaspoon drained, chopped
   capers

3 cloves garlic, peeled and
   minced

2 tablespoons balsamic
   vinegar

200ml (7fl oz) extra virgin
   olive oil

1. Use a mortar and pestle to
   combine the parsley, mint,
   anchovies and capers.
2. Add the garlic, vinegar and
   olive oil to the mixture,
   keeping it liquid. Add more
   oil if needed. Serve.

The problem for Lavazza and all the other coffee blenders in Italy, is that an incompetent waiter can make a pig's ear of even the finest blends. I'm sharing André's attention in Lavazza's tasting room with a group of managers from a British pizza chain, who are keen to learn the secrets of high quality espresso. André takes up his position on a sleek Gaggia worth several thousand pounds. 'It needs an expert to work it,' he insists, 'like a pilot in charge of an aeroplane.'

THE PERFECT CUP

'No order should take more than one minute,' André says. The best places for espresso are the busiest bars. There, the machine chugs out cup after miniscule cup, or *tazzina*, free of the oils that build up with infrequent use. André places a strainer beneath the funnel of an electric grinder, pulls its lever twice, packing it to the brim with fine grains of coffee, then twists it into the clamp of the espresso machine. The machine's pressure gauge approaches ten atmospheres as the water heats to an astonishing 93°C (200°F).

A *tazzina* is placed beneath one of the machine's funnels. André takes it from a line of preheated white porcelain cups. 'Never stack them up,' is the rule. 'The top ones get cold, and they are the first ones people use. They need to be warm to create the crema.' A button is switched on.

Tiny spots of coffee hit the bottom of the cup and seconds later it's over. 'Perfetto,' proclaims André. And he calls us closer to inspect his creation. The espresso is dark and thick beneath its hazelnut-coloured crema, the espresso's 'lid' of energetic foam that manages both to keep in the heat and prevent the release of aroma before tasting. 'Two mouthfuls, maximum,' André instructs. No problem. Downed in one. Perfetto indeed.

Above: A mouth-watering array of pastries is always on display in the Caffè Torino.

Right: A boy, dwarfed by the Caffè Torino's counter, delights in a traditional breakfast *cornetto*.

Opposite: Shoppers stroll through the city's elegant porticoes.

Zabaglione

Egg yolks and Marsala

A supremely rich dish, and one found throughout the Italian peninsula, zabaglione's popularity in Turin is due to the many Torinese of southern descent whose forebears moved to the great industrial city to escape the poverty of the South. Marsala, the sweet dessert wine of Sicily, is a common ingredient, but for a taste of real authenticity, add some strega, the thick, syrupy Italian liqueur that's a staple of bars from Rome south. According to the great food writer Elizabeth David, Italian doctors even go so far as to claim restorative powers for zabaglione!

Ingredients

6 egg yolks

100g (3oz) caster sugar

250ml (9fl oz) dry Marsala wine or Strega

amaretti biscuits to serve

1. Beat the egg yolks with the sugar until pale
2. Add the Marsala or Strega and pour the mixture into a large bowl that you have placed over a pan of simmering water.
3. Beat the mixture until a thick foam is created.
4. Serve in warmed glasses with forest fruits and amaretti biscuits, and topped with crumbled amaretti biscuits.

Torta di cioccolata

Chocolate cake

That the Torinese have a sweet tooth is beyond question. The chocolates they produce are overpoweringly, unashamedly rich, and to be eaten only in small quantities. The chocolate cake is a perfect example of the way the Piedmontese took the fruit of the New World and made it a northern European classic and a mainstay of cafe society.

Ingredients

100g (4oz) high quality dark chocolate

50g (2oz) unsalted butter

2 medium eggs, separated

100g (4oz) sugar

1 tablespoon flour

1. Melt the chocolate and the butter in a bowl placed over a pan of simmering water.

2. In a food processor, mix the egg yolks with the sugar and the flour. Add the melted chocolate and butter mixture and combine well.

3. Beat the egg whites until stiff and fold them into the mixture by hand.

4. Pour the chocolate mixture into a buttered and floured 30cm (12in) loose-bottomed baking tin and bake in the oven at 135°C (275°F) gas mark 1 for 45 minutes.

5. Allow the cake to cool in the baking tin before carefully unmoulding.

CHAPTER 2: VENICE

REINVENTING TRADITION

You eat worse in Venice than anywhere else in Italy. And more expensively. So the cliché goes. However, like most clichés, there's some truth to it. The tacky streets that converge on Piazza San Marco and the city's railway station are filled with tourists eating their way through costly plates of chicken and chips or some other tasteless variant of the international style. But you can eat as well in Venice as any other city in Italy – and just as cheaply. It's not difficult to find a good – and good value – trattoria offering the city's distinctive and distinguished cuisine. But people regard Venice, the birthplace of modern tourism, as something of a fairytale location. Visitors can find it intimidating, too, with its crowded and labyrinthine layout, so they forget that ordinary people – about 60,000 of them – actually live here, and so cease to follow the golden rule of eating well: go where the locals go.

THE WORLD'S FINEST FISH MARKET

Venetians, after all, eat very well indeed. The Rialto market has operated from the same central site since 1097. Its pescaria, certainly the most famous and probably the best fish market in the world, is patronised almost entirely by knowledgeable residents, always eager to share their expertise, and a small core of regular visitors to Venice, returning to cook local fare in their rented apartments. Vegetables too are very good here, many of which are grown on the island of Sant'Erasmo: Venetians refer to the inhabitants of the island, which is larger than Venice proper but has a tiny population, as *gli matti*, the crazies. Their gene pool is famously shallow, the names Zanella and Vignotti being especially common. The label 'di Sant'Erasmo' is ubiquitous in Venetian shops and markets – and the island is especially famous for its purple artichokes, though all the vegetables in Venice seem a deeper, stronger colour than expected.

In the well-tramped parts of Venice, locals are hard to find. On the main island, the south-western district of Dorsoduro remains the most residential.

Opposite: Ruggiero Bovo, the unchallenged master of risotto alla buranella; gondolas; the pescaria or fish market.

Right: The superb produce of the island of Sant'Erasmo, the city's vegetable garden, on sale in the Rialto market.

HOLE IN THE WALL

Dorsoduro means 'hard back', reflecting the fact that its land is firmer than elsewhere in Venice, providing more stable foundations for building in this famously sinking city. The Gallerie dell'Accademia, the greatest of all Venetian art galleries – packed with masterpieces by the likes of Bellini, Titian and Tintoretto – is the usual entry point, over the Accademia bridge, for visitors to the district, and it is understandably stuffed with tourists every day. But behind it, in the centre and on the south side of Dorsoduro, daily life goes on pretty much undisturbed.

Tucked away in a high, brown-bricked alley, narrow even by Venetian standards, near the Piazza San Barnaba, where penniless eighteenth-century aristocrats – the barnabotti – were once provided with cheap housing by the declining Republic, stands Osteria Vini Padovani. It doesn't appear to be much more than a hole in the wall, but it is big enough inside for four or five tables, each of which sports classic, checkerboard linen. Many of its customers, mainly men and

some students, stand at the bar, drinking a glass of wine – *un'ombra* in the local dialect – snacking on cicheti, the Venetian take on tapas, that might include anything from olives, ham and bread, to strange, local specialities such as bits of nervetti (boiled veal cartilage) or musetto (pig's intestines spiced and filled with ham). The Venetians like their flavours strong. To those who sit down, the family – a young woman, a young man, and their father – serve classic, basic and very palatable Venetian dishes of which fegato alla Veneziana is the most famous. Everything is cooked in a forbidding but cool kitchen tucked away within the high wall on the opposite side of the alley. 'We're one of the oldest osterias still going around here. We don't change much,' says the son.

It may come as a surprise to many that this most romantic of cities delights in the decidedly unromantic combination of liver and onions, but that's what fegato alla Veneziana is. It's an easy one to cook if – and this is true of so much Italian food – one has access to the right ingredients, in this case very tender calves' liver and fresh onions. The key to the dish's success is the contrast in the way the two ingredients are cooked. The roughly chopped onions are sweated very slowly in a little olive oil for about half an hour, their natural sweetness enhanced. The savoury liver is thinly sliced and flash-fried in two or three minutes. It's often served with the strikingly white polenta that comes down to the city from the corn-growing region of Friuli, where the Latin world meets the Slavonic. The congeniality of the two main ingredients' very different textures is immediately obvious and not confined to Venice, as any resident of the north of England – where liver and onions has long been a favourite dish – will tell you.

Other Venetian classics on offer in Vini Padovani include salt cod stewed slowly in milk, and seppie in nero or cuttlefish cooked in its own ink and traditionally served with spaghetti, though pasta is something of an afterthought in Venetian cuisine. Cheap but not unpalatable wine from the nearby, hugely productive region of the Veneto, served by the carafe, accompanies all.

Above and far left: The most photographed grocer in the world mans the fruit barge moored permanently near Campo San Barnaba in the district of Dorsoduro, one of the more residential areas of the main island. Sant'Erasmo tomatoes are a local speciality.

Left: Osteria Vini Padovani, tucked away in Dorsoduro's backstreets, is one of the custodians of traditional Venetian cuisine.

Fegato alla Veneziana

Venetian liver

Venetians are fans of offal, a fact reflected in their pragmatic approach to meat. This superb dish is entirely dependent on the ways in which the two elements are cooked. The onions are slowly sweated, while the liver is cooked in a flash of heat.

Ingredients

6 tablespoons olive oil
2 large onions, roughly chopped
450g (1lb) calves liver
2 tablespoons chopped, flat-leaf parsley

1. Heat half the oil in a pan and add the onion. Cover and cook for about half an hour, stirring occasionally.

2. When the onions are soft and golden, heat the remaining oil in another pan and fry the liver very quickly on both sides. (This will take less than 5 minutes.)

3. Place the liver and onions on a serving dish and sprinkle with freshly chopped parsley.

BEST SEAFOOD RISOTTO IN THE WORLD?

It's clear from a visit to Vini Padovani that most traditional Venetian dishes have not spread far beyond the city. There is one exception. Two million Milanese might not agree, but Venice is home to the best risotto in the world; it's the city and the lagoon's archetypal dish. Milan's dry, meaty variety is more consistent, but when the fluid, seafood risottos of the lagoon are made by a master, they are sublime. After all, the Venetian Republic held the Po valley, the greatest, most productive of Europe's rice-growing regions within its grasp for centuries.

In my opinion the best risotto in Venice is made in Burano, an island in the northern lagoon, a traditional fishing community where houses are painted in the brightest of colours to distinguish them to their seaborne owners from the distance of the sea. Burano, a 45-minute trip from Venice itself, gets its fair share of tourists, but the vast majority settle for a circuit of the main piazza, named after Baldassare Galuppi, the eighteenth-century composer who was born here, and ignore the rest.

Burano is fashionable of late, slowly attracting the attention of artists and designers. Trattoria al Gatto Nero, the Black Cat, is the one substantial restaurant on the south of the island. Elton John, a sometime Venetian resident, eats there. Philippe Starck lives opposite.

But this is no chic Eurotrash hang out for celebrities, nor is it an intimidating experience for those of us less well endowed with wealth and fame. It's an uncompromising, unpretentious place, especially popular with residents of Venice proper, and from whose tiny kitchen spring many of the wonders of Venetian cuisine. Its seafood risotto — risotto alla buranella — is a dish, simple in execution, rich and complex in taste, that is worthy of pilgrimage.

Above and right: Trattoria al Gatto Nero, the 'black cat', Burano's finest eaterie, looks out onto the island's busy canal.

Radicchio rosso
Red winter lettuce

Radicchio is at its best in the weeks running up to Christmas, and is wonderful eaten raw when deepest red. It is especially good when combined with fennel. This dish is a fine example of the pungent flavours for which the Veneto is famous, and is generally eaten on its own, with no accompaniment.

Ingredients

100g (4oz) pancetta or speck
2 cloves garlic
750g (1lb 10oz) radicchio
4 small onions
1 tablespoon olive oil

1. Roughly chop the pancetta or speck, then peel and thinly slice the garlic. Roughly chop the radicchio and the four onions.

2. Heat the olive oil and sauté the garlic and chopped pancetta or speck. After a couple of minutes add the radicchio and the roughly chopped onions. Mix well for 5 minutes then serve.

'Burano is not like it was 25 years ago' – not least because its colourful fish market that stood opposite the Gatto Nero was closed down by EU rulings. 'How can a fish that's still wriggling be a hygiene problem?'

Massimo Bovo

Previous page: Chef Ruggiero and fisherman Salvado display the gò, key ingredient of the Gatto Nero's risotto.

Below: When the Gatto Nero closes, its entire staff gather round the kitchen table to crack open the day's haul of crabs.

Below: Fresh, near-transparent gamberini are a Venetian staple.

Opposite: Massimo Bovo at work.

CATCH OF THE DAY

I arrive at the Gatto Nero at midday on a Saturday in June. Even the locals think it hot. Massimo, son of the owner Ruggiero, meets me under the restaurant's colourful canopy. A woman paces alongside us with her grandson in her arms, sheltering in the shade. A fisherman, Salvado, has just arrived at the kitchen with his day's catch in a carrier bag. Massimo buys the lot: there's gò, the Venetian name for a fish that resembles a plump little sea bass; sea bass itself; spider crabs; crayfish; octopus and scampi, the word Venetians gave the world to describe shellfish.

A tiny crab, no bigger than a fingernail, crawls over the collection. 'Next year, that'll be a molecha,' says Massimo, referring to the small, soft-shelled crabs that when fried are a Venetian delicacy. Everything is brought in fresh by Salvado, who now sits outside in the shade smiling and clasping a large, cold glass of Sans Souci beer – the perfect drink for the heat. All but the octopus must be eaten on the day it's delivered – the octopus has two days' grace. 'You can't mess people about. After a day, the cats get the fish. Most restaurants will keep feeding customers with it. But people know, you know.'

'This used to be an old fisherman's haunt,' says Massimo, pointing to the inside of the restaurant. 'Men playing cards, that kind of stuff. Then my father took it over – he's half self-taught, shall we say? We've always insisted that the tourists should have the same stuff as the locals, who tend to be Venetian anyway. Burano people tend to be a bit funny. They'll turn up for christenings, but not much else. They don't really like going out to eat.'

'Where do you get your ingredients from?' I ask. 'The fishermen. There's a network of them we trust, all of them local. What they bring we cook. Sometimes they shout from the canal "What do you want?" and I'll shout back "What have you got?"'

REINVENTING TRADITION

The cramped kitchen is an inferno, the cooks stripped down to their vests. All except Ruggiero, who looks cool – in every sense – in his full chef's regalia, hat included, despite the fact that a huge metal pan of spaghetti alle vongole is simmering away, only adding to the stifling heat. 'People say you make the best risotto in Venice,' I say to him. 'It's true,' he says, modestly. I'll show you how, I promise.' Trust is a word Venetians use a lot. The best restaurants in *La Serenissima*, use menus only to attract the conservative diner. 'You have to put yourself in my hands,' says Massimo. 'Do you trust me? If not, then go and eat somewhere else, have spaghetti e pomodoro. You won't be happy here.' My trust in Massimo is amply rewarded.

Before Ruggiero gives me a lesson in risotto making, Massimo brings a long procession of freshly cooked seafood, all of it utterly fresh and delicious. I'd seen it all wriggling just an hour or so before: tiny scallops cooked in butter; cuttlefish milk, which looks like the white flesh of a little eel, but which has the rubbery consistency of squid; mullet cooked bacalao-style, poached in milk; a dressed granseola, or spider crab; gamberini or crayfish, cannochia or squill; a flat prawn, and a baby octopus. Prosecco – a light, dry white wine – washes it down.

Making a
seafood risotto:

1. Ruggiero uses
an extra virgin olive
oil from a supplier
in Umbria.

2. Heads of garlic
are pressed into the
oil then discarded.

3. Fresh gò are
selected then added
to the fragrant oil.

4. Onions and
celery are added to
the saucepan.

'This used to be an old fisherman's haunt,' says Massimo, pointing to the inside of the restaurant. 'Playing cards, that kind of stuff. Then my father took it over.'

Massimo Bovo

5. Ruggiero presses the mixture down into a sieve, and collects the juice in another pan. The solids are then discarded.

6. Ruggiero uses Carnaroli or Vialone Nano rice for his risotto.

7. The rice is cooked in the stock.

8. Ruggiero tastes the stock for his classic risotto.

Risotto alla Buranella

Seafood risotto from Burano

Ruggiero Bovo, the masterchef of Burano's celebrated
Trattoria al Gatto Nero, makes this dish with small, fleshy
fish called gò that are local to the lagoon. Small sea bass
can be used instead. The dish itself, like most Italian
classics, is a simple one but dependent on the best
ingredients. The rice should be top quality Carnaroli or
Vialone Nano, the olive oil extra virgin, the butter 'white'
and preferably Italian: Beppino Occelli's marvellous creamy
butter is now quite widely available in Europe – it's the
same one employed by Ruggiero to add a lustrous sheen.

Ingredients

extra virgin olive oil

450g (1lb) of small sea bass,
  monkfish, or white fish

1 large peeled white onion

2 sticks celery

2 cloves garlic

1 teaspoon chopped,
  flat-leaf parsley

350g (12oz) Carnaroli or Vialone
  Nano rice

50g (2oz) butter

50g (2oz) Parmesan cheese

1. To make the stock, cover the bottom of a large pan with olive oil and add the fish, whole or filleted, plus the whole onion and celery and stir. After 2 or 3 minutes, fill the pan almost to the top with boiling water. Add the flat-leaf parsley, and simmer for 10 minutes.

2. Empty the contents into a sieve placed over another pan and press down on the fish and vegetables to release their juice. Discard the solids.

3. Cover the bottom of another pan with olive oil, then add the rice and a ladle of stock to cover it. Bring to a simmer, and add more stock when necessary, keeping the rice moist but never runny.

4. Continue the process until all the stock has been absorbed. When the rice is al dente, add the butter then the Parmesan to bind it. Serve immediately.

We're joined at the table by Julia, Massimo's Scottish-born wife of eight years, who has been working throughout a hot, demanding lunchtime in the kitchen. The lunchtime customers drift away and Massimo lights up a cigarette. 'We're trying to evolve here. Burano is not like it was 25 years ago' – not least because its colourful fish market that stood opposite the Gatto Nero was closed down by EU rulings on hygiene. 'How can a fish that's still wriggling be a hygiene problem?' Massimo protests. 'We don't want it to be like it was 25 years ago, but we do care about its traditions. We're reinventing them. We are the best guardians of those traditions, because we know them best.'

Above: Father and son, Ruggiero and Massimo Bovo relax after another exhausting, exacting lunchtime at the Gatto Nero.

Risi e bisi

Rice and peas

The name is prosaic, but this dish has been a Venetian
staple for centuries. It makes the most of the high-quality
sweet, fresh peas that are brought in spring to the Rialto
market from the fertile fields of Sant'Erasmo. Shelled at
the last minute, they are boiled in the same water as the
rice, which imparts to it a delicate, grassy flavour. As
with all Italian rice dishes, use the best rice you can
find: Arborio, or even better, Carnaroli or Vialone Nero.
Unlike the rice dishes of Milan and Lombardy, this one
should retain ample moisture.

Ingredients

50g (2oz) butter

1 tablespoon olive oil

1 medium onion, chopped

2 slices pancetta, chopped

250g (10oz) petits pois (fresh
are best, but frozen will do)

1.5 litres (2 ½ pints) chicken
stock

250g (10oz) Arborio rice

5 tablespoons grated
Parmesan cheese

1 tablespoon chopped
flat-leaf parsley

1. Melt half the butter in the
olive oil over a medium heat
and sauté the onion and the
pancetta. Add the petits
pois, cover with some of the
stock and simmer for about
10 minutes.

2. Add the rice and the rest of
the stock, and simmer slowly
to reduce the liquid.

3. When the rice is al dente,
add the remaining butter and
the cheese to firm it up.
Garnish with parsley and
serve immediately.

YOU CAN'T BUY THIS STUFF

My lesson in making risotto is proof of that. Ruggiero, having barely broken sweat after his exertions in the kitchen, takes a deep metal pan and covers its base with a layer of olive oil. 'It's the best,' he says. 'From where Umbria borders Tuscany. They supply it direct. You can't buy this stuff, but good extra virgin olive oil will do.' He then puts three whole garlic cloves in, colours them, then discards them. In goes the gò, which he gilds in the oil, along with two peeled, whole white onions, and three stalks of celery. After a while, he adds two litres of water. Peppered, the mix simmers for 10 to 15 minutes. Then Ruggiero sieves the mixture into a shallower pan, pressing every last bit of liquid from the sieve. 'This is the stock for the risotto' says Ruggiero. 'The greener the better.'

The choice of rice is crucial. 'Carnaroli, tre punte, is perfect,' Ruggiero declares, pointing to the shape of the rice grain, spade-like with three white points at one end. Rice is added to the pan, and covered in a film of olive oil. 'That gives it a little bite.' Then the stock is added slowly, as Ruggiero stirs with a wooden spoon, taking the odd sip of stock. A little salt is added, a bit more pepper, some basil. The process continues until Ruggiero judges the rice cooked. Then he adds a rectangle of cold, fresh butter and a handful of Parmesan cheese 'to give it body.' The taste is complex but subtle. The best risotto imaginable.

Above, right: Venice remains a working city, its canals the arteries of its economy.

Centre: The quality of the Rialto market's produce is matched by its majestic location in the heart of Venice.

Right: Diners enjoy traditional Venetian cuisine just a few streets away from the tourist crush.

Overleaf: The brightly painted houses of Burano's are designed to be visible from the sea.

Tiramisù

'Pick me up'

Sugar, or 'Indian salt', first came to Europe through the
port of Venice, as did coffee. The two combine with alcohol
in what is probably the finest of all Italian desserts.

Ingredients

2 tablespoons rum or dry
  Marsala wine

4 tablespoons espresso coffee

1 tablespoon grappa

12 sponge fingers

250g (10oz) mascarpone cheese

1 egg, separated

2 tablespoons icing sugar

30g (1oz) melted dark chocolate

1. Mix half the rum or Marsala
   with the coffee and grappa.

2. Arrange the sponge fingers
   in a small tin just big
   enough to fit them in a row.
   Drizzle the rum mixture
   evenly over the fingers.

3. Beat the mascarpone, egg
   yolk and icing sugar
   together, then add the rest
   of the rum or Marsala. Beat
   the egg white and fold it
   into the mascarpone mixture.

4. Spoon the mixture over the
   sponge fingers, then drizzle
   the chocolate over the
   dessert. Chill in the fridge
   for 24 hours before serving.

CHAPTER 3: PARMA

A RICH LAND

Parma is an undeniably elegant city. It is also one of the wealthiest in Italy, and generally considered to have the highest quality of living anywhere in a country that's not short of *la dolce vita*. The region that surrounds it is home to Ferrari, Lamborghini and Maserati, bywords for cutting-edge car design and complex, brilliant engineering. But most of its wealth is founded on more traditional products, two of which have made this compact, cultured city (the home of Italy's greatest opera composer Giuseppe Verdi and the conductor Arturo Toscanini) famous throughout the world. One is Parmigiano-Reggiano, the delicate, crumbly grano cheese, that is the traditional accompaniment to so many Italian dishes at home and abroad. The other is prosciutto: Parma's translucent cured ham. Both are the products of patience and skill.

A CULTURED CUISINE

Parma shares the Appian Way, the long Roman road that cuts through the northern province of Emilia, with other great cities noted for their culture and cuisine: Bologna, Reggio-Emilia, Modena. But Parma is the most immediately striking city, visually stunning but never overreaching itself. The Piazza del Duomo, which holds Parma's cathedral and Benedetto Antelami's egg yolk-coloured baptistery, is — in my view — the most beautiful Romanesque square in a land filled with architectural treasures.

Opposite: A dog enjoys a saucer of the milk that goes to make Parmesan; a Parmigiano-Reggiano begins to take shape; cycling past Parma's Romanesque baptistery.

Above, right: Antelami's baptistery merges with the cathedral in Parma's Piazza Duomo .

Right: A cow of the Holsten breed, one of the four providers of milk for Parmesan cheese.

'Everyone here is very proud of what we do. In the end, we just want to be perfect. It's a very difficult task, which never ends. Every day of every year we follow the same process. It never changes, there is never a day off, the cows never stop producing milk.'

Antonio Quelli

Above: The afternoon milking of cows in a farm belonging to the Consorzio.

Right: Dairy farmer Antonio Quelli and friend take a break.

Opposite: A newly cut drum of perfectly matured Parmesan cheese. It never tastes quite so good again.

Cristiana Clerici, a local woman who works for the consortium of Parmesan cheese producers, says 'It is a beautiful city, Parma, but you have to try so hard to keep up with the fashions. It's exhausting. Everyone here is so concerned about the way they look.' I follow her by car out of what is, by Italian standards at least, an unusually friendly environment for cyclists and pedestrians, into the fertile countryside that envelops the city. Her mission: to show me how Parmesan cheese is produced.

South-east of the city, in the unremarkable village of Basilicagoiano, is the wide, low premises of Latteria Social San Stefano, one of almost 600 producers of Parmigiano-Reggiano cheese in an area that extends far beyond the environs of Parma, to include the provinces of Modena and Reggiano – hence the product's hyphenated name – and even reaching as far as Mantua and Bologna.

Anolini

Pasta filled with beef and red wine

MAKES ABOUT 20 ANOLINI

The traditional mainstay of Sunday lunch in Parma, this variant on ravioli is filled with stracotto, a slowly cooked, rich stew for which the province is famous.

For the stracotto

250g (10oz) butter
1 medium carrot, finely chopped
1 medium onion, finely chopped
half a stick celery, finely chopped
450g (1lb) lean minced beef
1 Cotechino sausage, finely diced or 450g (1lb) pork sausage meat
1 tablespoon tomato purée
1 glass red wine
85g (3oz) fresh breadcrumbs
50g (2oz) grated Parmesan
2 medium eggs
pinch of nutmeg

1. Gently melt the butter in an ovenproof casserole. Brown the vegetables.
2. Add the meat, and cook for 10 minutes, stirring with a wooden spoon.
3. Add the tomato purée and the wine and bring to the boil.
4. Cover the casserole and place in an oven preheated to 150°C (300°F) gas mark 2. Cook for 3 to 5 hours, stirring occasionally, until reduced and thickened.
5. Combine the remaining ingredients in a separate bowl, then add to the filling. Leave to cool.

For the pasta

250g (10oz) plain, unbleached flour
3 medium eggs
1 teaspoon grated nutmeg

1. Make a mound of flour on your work surface and make a well at the centre.
2. Pour the eggs into the well and add the nutmeg.
3. Stir the eggs together with your finger, then gradually work the eggs into the flour until a dough forms.
4. Knead the dough for about 10 to 15 minutes.
5. Roll out the dough as thinly as possible (it should be almost transparent), adding flour to keep it from sticking to the board.
6. Cut the pasta into 2 same-size sheet. Put teaspoonfuls of the filling on 1 sheet of the rolled-out pasta at about 4cm (1 ½ in) intervals.
7. Cover with the remaining sheet of pasta, and cut out small rounds about 4cm (1 ½ in) diameter with a pastry cutter. Pinch the edges firmly together.

TO COOK:
1. Bring a large pan of salted water to the boil.
2. Add the anolini, return to the boil and cook for about 30 seconds.
4. Remove carefully with a slotted spoon and serve with melted butter and Parmesan.

1. Master cheesemaker, Pietro Lelli, tests the curd's consistency.

2. A worker uses a *spino* to shatter the curds that form in the vat.

3. The mass of cheese is wrapped in hemp and attached to a dowel.

THE MEN IN WHITE

The making of Parmesan is both an art and a science, though the cool, sterile, white interiors of the creamery in which the cheese is produced, suggest only the latter discipline. Soon after dawn, a tanker full of the morning's fresh milk arrives in the yard of San Stefano. The milk is blended with milk from the previous evening that has been allowed to separate naturally from its cream (which is then used to make butter). The blend is pumped into the dairy's 26 *caldiere* or copper-lined iron cauldrons, which look like inverted church bells, under the supervision of Pietro Lelli, San Stefano's master cheesemaker.

Fermenting whey from the previous day's production is added, and the vats are heated to 26°C (78°F). As it heats up, rennet from the stomachs of nursing calves is also added, and in 8 to 12 minutes, the mixture coagulates, and the curd begins to form. Pietro and his small team of men, who are dressed all in white, even down to their boots, continually feel and touch the contents of the vats. 'We must have contact with the product,' Pietro insists, crumbling the curd in his fingers as he tests its consistency.

Once a sufficient amount of curdling has taken place, Pietro and his men take a *spino*, or 'branch', which is in reality a giant steel whisk, and shatter the curds into fragments the size of wheat or rice grains. Hence the term 'grano' in describing the family of cheeses to which Parmesan belongs. The vats are then heated for another half an hour, to 56°C (133°F), at which temperature the curds fuse into a single mass. They are then left to cool.

4. The cheese, wrapped in fresh cloth, is placed in a circular plastic mould, or *fascera*.

5. Left to dry, the cheese is imprinted with its 'birth certificate': its time and place of origin.

6. Inspector Sergio Giuberti 'drums' the cheese to reveal any ulcerations. This one is perfect.

Once set, two men use an enormous wooden paddle to scoop up the mass that has formed at the bottom of the cauldron, divide it into two, wrap each half in sheets tied to a wooden dowel, and leave them to drain over the vat. The whey will be fed to the pigs that produce prosciutto.

Once drained, each cheese is carried like a jungle prisoner into an adjacent room by two men. It is pressed by a heavy wooden disc, wrapped in a new sheet of hemp, then placed in a circular plastic mould, or *fascera*. It is turned three or four times a day to prevent humidity concentrating in one place. A little later, a stamp is inserted between the cheesecloth and the mould, imprinting through a matrix of dots the words 'Parmigiano-Reggiano', the number of the creamery, and the month and year of its production.

The turning and drying continues in the same dim, cool room for two or three days. Salting follows. The cheese, still wrapped in hemp, is immersed in saline solution for 22 days, and again turned regularly. The warehouses that contain the vast steel baths of cheese are dark, silent, unpopulated. So are the warehouses where the cheese is taken to be stored for an average of two years. Unpopulated that is, except for three days of the year, when the white-jacketed inspectors of the Consorzio del Formaggio Parmigiano-Reggiano arrive. The Consorzio, or consortium, was founded in 1934, to guarantee the quality of a style of cheese that has barely changed in style and substance since the fourteenth century. Certainly, Boccaccio describes it in the *Decameron*: 'There was a mountain of grated Parmesan cheese, over which people stood who did nothing but make macaroni and ravioli.' The standing, the watching continues.

THE OPENING CEREMONY

The ageing room of a dairy is a remarkable sight: as many as 15,000 wheels of cheese lie stacked on shelves that reach to within a hand's grasp of the ceiling. Constantino, one of two inspectors, is near the very top. He's stamping year-old wheels of cheese that have made the grade with the distinctive oval brand of the Consorzio. Each wheel of cheese is taken down from its place on the shelf, and held sideways on a stool-like table. Tapping out a rhythm over its surface, the inspector can tell if the cheese is ulcerated, diseased, hollowed in some way. This batch is fine.

Sandro, son of the master cheesemaker Pietro, is given the honour of opening a wheel to examine it more closely. He takes a short, rather blunt chisel specially made for the task, and cuts into the thick rind. Eventually, the wheel splits in half, revealing a crumbly, crystalline interior that glints even in the ageing room's low light. 'This is the perfect moment,' says Sandro. 'It never tastes better than it does now.' Everyone reaches over to take a piece, to taste again a flavour they have known all their lives. I too take a shard of the cheese, which is vulnerable from now on to oxidation. To say it melts in the mouth is not to talk metaphorically. It does just that. The peptides, peptones and amino acids that are the scientific explanation of Parmesan's uniqueness, reveal themselves to the palate in its paradoxical combination of crunchy smoothness. It is perfect. The best of these wheels will be returned to the shelves to age for another two years to become *stravecchio*, the oldest, and best of all Parmesan.

Right: A factory worker cuts drums of Parmesan, creating portions for Europe's supermarkets.

'This is the perfect moment,' he says. 'It never tastes better than it does now.' Everyone reaches over to take a piece, even though they've tasted it all their lives.

Sandro Lelli

Left: A special moment. Sandro Lelli cuts a drum of Parmigiano-Reggiano to reveal the delicate shards of cheese, above.

Asparagi al Parmigiano

Grilled asparagus with Parmesan

Almost 2,000 years ago, the Roman poet Martial celebrated the asparagus of Emilia-Romagna. The province of Ravenna in particular, is said to produce the finest in Italy and, therefore, the world. Parma contributes the cheese whose nutty, crystalline texture blends so well with the fibrous asparagus once it has been softened by the grill's flames.

Olive oil, though strongly associated with the Italian diet, is usually spurned in Parma whose inhabitants, like those of its near neighbours Bologna and Modena, prefer to cook with butter and cream. But in this case, a light drizzle of extra virgin olive oil adds a richness to the combination.

Ingredients

16 asparagus spears
extra virgin olive oil
Parmesan cheese

1. Place the asparagus on a preheated grill pan and drizzle with the oil. Alternatively, coat with olive oil and cook on medium-hot griddle.
2. When the asparagus is seared, remove it from the grill or griddle pan.
3. Serve with shaved Parmesan.

Scaloppina alla Marsala

Veal escalope with Marsala

The Italians, an unsqueamish bunch when it comes to food, love veal. The Bolognese add cheese to it, the people of Parma sometimes wrap it in their ham. They also cook it with Marsala, the syrupy sweet wine that originates in the eponymous Sicilian port. Apparently, it's not unlike the wine the Romans drank.

The rich flavour of the Marsala wine blends well with both the butter in which the meat is cooked, and the juices that emanate from it. This dish goes particularly well with porcini mushrooms, or French cep – a reminder that Parma's cuisine is strongly influenced by that of France.

Ingredients

1 tablespoon olive oil

30g (1oz) butter

4 veal escalopes, each about
  175g (6oz)

plain flour

125ml (4fl oz) dry Marsala

1. Heat the oil and half the butter in a frying pan.
2. Lightly coat the escalopes with flour and sauté rapidly until both sides are brown.
3. Add the Marsala, cook for 2 minutes, then remove the veal from the pan.
4. Reduce the sauce, add the remaining butter and pour the sauce over the veal.

A LONG, SLOW PROCESS

Langhirano, a small but noticeably affluent town 15 kilometres to the south of Parma, is characterised by the imposing warehouses, peppered with tall, rectangular, shuttered windows, that stand on every corner. All the windows face the same direction, south to north. The reason? This is where the ham, famous throughout the world as prosciutto di Parma, is prepared, and the windows are aligned to catch the sweet, dry air from the Apennines that give the hams their distinctive taste as they hang and age in the warehouse galleries.

Like the cheese warehouses, the curing galleries are sparsely populated. Just 20 people work in these vast spaces, which are cavernous and cool in contrast to the heat outside. And, again like the cheese, the creation of Parma ham is a slow, gradual process in which time is a key component. Nothing is rushed here.

Preserving ham through salting dates back centuries. The Roman statesman Cato wrote of the process in the first century BC. But the Consorzio del Prosciutto di Parma, with its famous five-pronged ducal crown, was set up only in 1963, to guarantee the quality of its output, and maintain the distinctive style and flavour of its prized product. Paolo Tramelli, one of the Consorzio's spokesmen and my guide, is chirpy after a major legal victory over a British supermarket chain denied the right to package the ham of Parma.

Above: It's not all ham and cheese. A street trader proffers fresh fruit to the Parmigiani.

Opposite: Parma ham, marked with its distinctive ducal crown, ages in the warehouse.

Left: Warehouse workers massage and salt hams before they are hung once more.

Below: Parma ham is served thinly sliced. Ham slicers are ubiquitous in Parma's kitchens.

Opposite: A chain-mail glove offers some protection when de-boning the fully aged ham.

The legs must arrive within three days of slaughter. Weighing 14 to 15 kilograms when they arrive, the curing process will reduce that weight by almost a third. First of all, each ham is massaged; it used to be done by hand, but machines do it now, taking out the blood, and lengthening the muscle fibres. A master salter, of which there's one in each company, prepares a mixture of dry and humid sea salt that is spread carefully on each ham. 'He's the most important person in the entire process,' Paolo informs me. The ham is stored for seven days at high humidity (75 per cent or so), salted again, and stored for 15 to 18 days. The tattoo of the breeding farm and slaughterhouse is added, as is the marker PP – 'per Parma'. The residual salt is removed, and the ham is hung for three months at the same temperature, but at 65 per cent humidity.

'THAT'S WHAT YOU PAY FOR'

Pio Tosini is a medium-sized warehouse, producing something like 100,000 hams a year. Whereas hams produced elsewhere are those of six-month-old pigs weighing 100 kilograms, the pigs of Parma must be at least ten months old, by which time they've reached half as much weight again. 'That last four months is expensive,' says Paolo. 'That's a lot of what you pay for.' You also pay for a remarkable attention to detail, and a quality control system that verges on the fanatical.

The pigs, from three breeds – Large White, Landrance and Durac – come from over 5,500 farms throughout Northern and Central Italy. The local workers provide the know-how that transforms good quality hams into great ones.

'That's the most dangerous job of all – de-boning the ham. It's left till last. You can lose your hand in the process. That's why the man wears a chainmail glove.'

Paolo Tramelli

The hams are washed of their salt crystals with warm water and moved to one of the windowed galleries that contain thousands of hams. They hang here for a further three months on special wooden frames called *scalere*. (They looked to me like weeping tears of prosciutto, so grand was the scale.) When it rains, the windows are closed, when it is temperate, the windows are opened. The whole process is carefully monitored and controlled.

Taken down, the hams are beaten into a rounder, fuller shape and seasoned with minced pig fat, salt, pepper, even a little ground rice. The mixture is spread smoothly over the skin to keep the hams moist. They're then moved to cellars for a further three months, where little air and light penetrates. Inspectors check the quality of each ham with a horse bone needle called a *spillatura* that absorbs the fragrance of the ham for a very brief moment. When it passes a series of tests relating to size, fat, age and lack of blemish, it is fire-branded with the Consorzio's crown.

Almost to the end, the process is characterised by its patient, tender care. But de-boning the finished ham requires not only skill, but a great deal of violence. The *sgorbia*, the de-boning instrument, is a fearful looking piece of jagged metal, and even the man who wields it – in a little ante-chamber to the series of warehouses – wears a chainmail glove to save his hand if he makes a slip. It's an unexpectedly dramatic coda to the process.

Right: Preparing the Zoni cows for their afternoon milking. The Consorzio's cows are allowed to feed on grass and hay only.

Opposite: Slicing prosciutto di Parma in a splendidly stocked shop: the Salumeria Gardoni in Torrechiara.

IT'S NOT JUST HAM AND CHEESE

Paolo and I travel to the neighbouring town of Torrechiara, which stands in the shade of a splendidly preserved fifteenth-century castle, the work of Pier Maria Rossi, a renaissance polymath. Its four imposing towers, and double set of walls, can be seen from miles away. The town's square is sleepy except for the splendid Salumeria Gardoni, who rustle up a plate each of Prosciutto di Parma and Parmigiano-Reggiano, and a bottle of a slightly sparkling local wine made of Malvasia grapes. 'Put a little butter on the ham,' says Paolo. 'That's how we locals eat it.' I don't know how many times Paolo has eaten this combination, but he seems as excited by its simple prospect as I am. 'Do you ever get bored of ham and cheese?' I ask him. 'No,' he replies, a little surprised by my question. 'It's not just ham and cheese. It's Parma ham and Parmesan cheese.'

Fettucine con prosciutto di Parma e panna

Fettucine with prosciutto and cream

This dish combines the two ingredients for which Parma is renowned – ham and cheese. Fettucine is the closest northern pasta-makers get to the wheaty, harder southern style.

Ingredients

400ml (14fl oz) double cream

100g (4oz) prosciutto cut into strips

85g (3oz) freshly grated Parmesan cheese

2 egg yolks

450g (1lb) fresh fettucine

1. Bring a large pan of salted water to the boil.
2. Mix the cream, ham, half the cheese and the egg yolks together in a bowl.
3. Place the bowl over a pan of simmering water and allow it to heat up while stirring from time to time. Do not allow the egg yolks to cook.
4. Meanwhile, cook the fettucine in the boiling water for 2 minutes or until al dente.
5. Drain the fettucine and add it to the sauce. Mix well and sprinkle the remaining Parmesan cheese over the pasta before serving.

Torta di riso
Rice cake

The *addobbi*, or 'decorations', are rowdy Emilian festivals, often taking place behind closed doors, which once had some religious justification, long forgotten. 'An *addobbo* without torta di riso, like a political banquet without speeches, cannot exist,' said one commentator.

Ingredients

1.2 litres (2 pints) milk

175g (6oz) Arborio rice

2 eggs, separated

140g (5oz) sugar

grated lemon rind of half a
    medium lemon

50g (2oz) candied citrus peel

4 tablespoons pine nuts

50g (2oz) toasted almonds, finely
    ground in a liquidiser

1 teaspoon vanilla essence

knob of butter

50g (2oz) fresh breadcrumbs

1. Bring the milk to the boil in a heavy saucepan.

2. Add the rice and simmer gently for half an hour until the milk has been absorbed. Leave to cool.

3. Beat the egg yolks and sugar and add the rice, rind, peel, pine nuts, almonds and vanilla essence. Beat the egg whites until stiff and gently stir them into the rice mixture.

4. Pour the mixture into a buttered 25cm (10in) diameter round tin and coat with breadcrumbs. Bake at 165°C (325°F) gas mark 3 for about 1 hour. Leave to cool.

CHAPTER 4: BOLOGNA

'LA GRASSA'

It either freezes or it burns in Bologna. In June, in a summer hot even by the standards of this cauldron of a city, it burns. 'E troppo caldo' is the constant refrain as temperatures climb to 37°C (98°F). They're the first words of Stefania Spisni, as she greets me around midday at her family's La Vecchia Scuola – the Old School – a restaurant and kitchen that practises and teaches the traditional ways of Bolognese cuisine. It's a fitting name. Alessandra, Stefania's mother, is as old school as they come, almost a stereotype of the traditional Italian Mamma: dressed in an ample, sleeveless, patterned dress, she is big, bold, hugely welcoming. Hers is plainly a life lived with gusto, and food is at its heart.

FAR FROM THE MEDITERRANEAN
It's a life of great certainties too. Alessandra's kitchen makes no concessions to modernity, nor to the food of any other region; her commitment is to the purest expression of Bolognese cuisine, which is regarded by many as the best Italy has to offer. But don't come here in search of the Mediterranean diet: olive oil and garlic are afterthoughts. Eggs, cheese, butter, lard, meat are ubiquitous. The greatest contribution of the Bolognese to Italian cuisine – and, for long now, that

Opposite: Bruno e Franco's fine food store; making pasta in Bruno and Franco's workshop; the railway station.

Above, left: Making tortellini by hand is skilled work.

Above, right: A nun seeks alms outside the Tamburini food store by Bologna's famous market.

of the world – is its pasta: tagliatelle, tortelloni, tortellini. Bologna's celebrated markets and food stores are stocked full with the corn-yellow colour of its fresh pasta. I'm here to learn how it's made. 'E semplice,' says Alessandra. We'll see. The ingredients are: just durum wheat, flour and eggs.

A STAR PERFORMER

Alessandra's kitchen is a spartan affair, hidden from the busy street on which it stands behind the blinds that guard it from the sun. Huge white tables dominate the front half of the kitchen, supporting wooden boards on which the pasta is prepared. The walls are tiled simply, Italian style. Stefania ensures everything is in place, like someone preparing the stage for a performance by a revered opera singer. After a few minutes, the star takes her place.

Alessandra creates a mound of flour in the middle of a huge board, and forms a crater, breaking half a dozen eggs within it. She works and works the mixture, increasing its elasticity, and forms a ball with it, about the size of her large hand. She rolls out the ball on the board with a formidable *materella*, the long rolling pin wielded by the expert pasta-maker. Again and again it is rolled and turned on the great wooden table until it is almost transparent against the light seeping through the kitchen window. This will be made into tortellini, the tiny, filled pasta loops traditionally served in broth. Stefania takes a roller with separate cutting wheels at regular intervals and drags it up and across the thin sheet of pasta. When she is finished, there are hundreds of tiny squares into which she places a fingernail-sized portion of filling. 'There's a little bit of chicken in there,' says Stefania, 'and mortadella of course' – the highly peppered, distinctly underrated Bolognese speciality of hashed pork sausage – 'plus some ham, Parmesan cheese – and *noci di moscato*,' the typically poetic Italian name for nutmeg. It's all bound together with eggs, about five of them for every pound of flour.

Above: Bologna's food markets are considered by many to be the finest in all Italy. The quality of their produce is unmatched.

Opposite: Alessandra Spisni holds the *materella* that she uses to transform pasta dough into almost transparent sheets.

1. Alessandra rolls out the sheets of pasta with a *materella* that's over a metre long .

2. The sheets are almost transparent by the time they are rolled out to the required thinness.

3. The sheets of pasta are then divided into small squares with a rolling cutter.

4

7

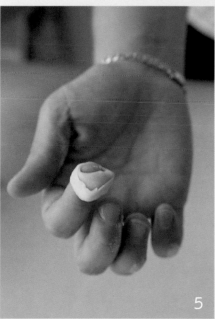

5

6

4. Each of the squares is packed with a spoonful of filling made of chicken, ham, sausage, Parmesan and nutmeg.

5. Each square is folded by hand, and wrapped delicately around a finger to produce tiny, perfect tortellini.

6. The consistency of the final product is remarkable considering that each pasta shape is made by hand.

7. The finished tortellini are stored in meshed drawers. Ideally, fresh egg pasta should be eaten within three days of making.

Each square is then folded by hand into a triangle, with one side's edge slightly lapping the other. The sides are then delicately pinched and folded round Stefania's petite index finger like a gold ring, until the two sides meet. She does this scores of times. She has done it tens of thousands of times before. The finished articles are placed on a wire mesh tray and stored in a cupboard. They must be eaten within three days.

'Could you use other kinds of fillings?' I ask Alessandra. 'Like spinach?' thinking of the mass-produced varieties of filled pasta found on supermarket shelves back home. She looks at me aghast. 'You could,' she says, 'but they wouldn't be Bolognese. In Parma, in Modena, they use spinach, artichokes, other things. But we use the meat mix you've just seen, or simply plain ricotta. If it's anything else, it may be fine, but it's not Bolognese.'

PERFECTION IN A BOWL

As we talk, Alessandra rolls out another sheet of pasta, rolling it around her *materella*, slipping it off and rolling it up like a newspaper. She takes an old knife, the *cullettino*, in her hand. 'This was my great-grandmother's, it was my mother's, and it will be my daughter's. From generation to generation it goes.' Its sharp edge slices thin wedges that curl into clumps of tagliolini, thin Bolognese pasta. 'What do you serve that with?' I ask. 'Butter.' 'Just butter?' 'Yes, just butter, about eight to ten grams of it. It has to be very good butter though,' pointing to the stark white slabs that come as a shock to any outsider who thinks butter is naturally yellow in colour.

Alessandra moves further inside the kitchen, to the domain of pots and pans that surround her stove. Water is bubbling away in a deep pan. She adds two great dollops of lard to the pan. A buzzer rings. An old friend enters, Salvatore, a Sicilian. We exchange the usual greetings as Alessandra, the lard having melted, scoops a little plastic beaker full of

She takes an old knife, the *cullettino*, in her hand. 'This was my great-grandmother's, it was my mother's, and it will be my daughter's. From generation to generation it goes.'

Alessandra Spisni

the broth she prepared the previous day in which the tortellini will be served. In a separate pan, the tortellini are blanched for a few seconds. 'When they're done, they should look like him,' she says, pointing to Salvatore, implying that he is wrinkled. He smiles.

She places the tortellini in a little dish and pours the broth over it. 'Just enough to cover it. See its wrinkles?' she says. Tortellini in brodo. Delicate, perfectly balanced, exquisitely spiced, the nutmeg just tangible above the piquant Parmesan and peppery mortadella. The pasta feels as though it cradles all the ingredients before letting them go gently onto the palate.

Alessandra takes out another ball of pasta dough and rolls it out, forming it once again into a 'newspaper'. She repeats the process as before, but this time the slices are thicker, forming tagliatelle, wide, flat pasta. Its traditional accompaniment is ragù, widely known elsewhere as Bolognese sauce, as in the ubiquitous spaghetti Bolognese. Ubiquitous everywhere but Bologna, of course; it has never occurred to anyone in Bologna that ragù could possibly be served with spaghetti. Spaghetti is a southern Italian invention, and is almost always sold dried.

The making of genuine ragù is a slow, laborious process. Its basic ingredients are the tomatoes for which Bologna and the surrounding province of Emilia-Romagna is famous, very finely minced beef (and occasionally pork), carrots, onions and celery. The cooking fat is pancetta, a bacon made from the stomach of Parma's pigs. Red wine is added too. It takes three hours to cook, though most Bolognese will keep the mixture in the fridge and reheat as required.

Opposite: Alessandra rolls up a pasta sheet then slices it to produce tagliolini.

Right: The fresh tortellini are blanched for barely a minute in a large pan of boiling water.

Tortellini in brodo

Fresh filled pasta in broth

Tortellini, often compared to the shape of a woman's navel, is the classic Bolognese pasta tirata: rolled, hand-made pasta. City archives dating back to the thirteenth century record the case of a young man breaking Bologna's night-time curfew. He was acquitted after explaining that he was trying to buy tortellini for some friends who had arrived unexpectedly.

For the filling

30g (1oz) chopped flat-leaf
   parsley
225g (8oz) ricotta cheese
85g (3oz) Parmesan cheese
1 egg yolk
grated nutmeg

1. Place all the ingredients in a mixing bowl and stir well.

For the pasta

250g (10oz) plain unbleached
   flour
3 medium eggs

1. Pour the flour into a mound on your work surface and make a well at the centre.

2. Pour the eggs into the well.

3. Stir the eggs together with your finger, then gradually work the eggs into the flour to make a dough.

4. Press the dough into a ball, and knead it well for 10 to 15 minutes.

5. Roll out the dough until the sheet is 3mm (¹⁄₈ in) thick, adding flour if necessary to prevent it sticking.

6. Using a pasta wheel, cut the dough into 1cm (¹⁄₂ in) squares, and put a dollop of filling on each square. Fold over the squares diagonally, and wrap each triangle around your index finger, squeezing the ends together to form the tortellini. Put them on a floured surface.

TO COOK:

1. Bring 1.2 litres (2 pints) of good chicken stock to a low simmer and carefully add the tortellini.

2. Cook gently for about 1 minute and then serve immediately in warmed bowls.

Right: Alessandra
prepares ragù, the
meat sauce made
from tomatoes and
minced beef that is
called 'Bolognese'
sauce elsewhere.

The simple meal is served in the garden with a traditional accompaniment of
prosciutto, the very dry bread of Bologna – called *crescenta* – and a glass of
slightly fizzy white wine, probably from the malvasia grape, and not a heavy red
wine one might expect to accompany such a dish. Indeed this is where commonly
made comparisons of Bolognese cuisine with that of Burgundy break down.
While a commitment to rich, hearty food is shared by both, drink is treated as
something of an afterthought by the Bolognese, as it is by most Italians. Wine
comes a long way behind food in the Italian imagination; the same could never
be said of the French, least of all the Burgundians.

I had eaten the tortellini in Alessandra's kitchen, as my desires overtook my
manners. The tagliatelle ragù is served on the glass table of the restaurant's
little garden. It is marked by subtlety, finesse and even – though this seems hard
to believe given the ingredients – its lightness. It's not at all heavy. The sauce
clings like sweat to the remarkably delicate pasta. Tortelloni of ricotta served in
a simple sauce finish off the meal. Three courses of pasta. Typically Bolognese.

In a separate pan, the
tortellini are blanched
for a few seconds. 'When
they're done, they should
look like him,' she says,
pointing to Salvatore.

Alessandra Spisni

Minestra di spinaci

Spinach soup

The spinach of northern Italy, perfected by specialist growers for over a thousand years is the best in the world. Gently spiced with that Bolognese favourite, nutmeg, this winter soup is a rough-edged treat.

Ingredients

675g (1½ lb) fresh spinach

50g (2oz) butter

grated nutmeg

250g (10oz) thawed frozen spinach

4 eggs

30g (1oz) grated Parmesan cheese

1.7 litres (3 pints) vegetable stock

1. Wash the fresh spinach and remove any tough stems.
2. Melt the butter in a pan and add the fresh spinach plus a pinch of grated nutmeg. Cover and cook over a low heat for 2 to 3 minutes.
3. Stir in the thawed spinach and cook for another minute.
4. Allow to cool a little, then chop in a food processor.
5. Beat the eggs and Parmesan cheese, then add to the spinach.
6. Bring the stock to the boil then take off the heat. Beat in the spinach until it turns creamy.

Ingredients

50g (2oz) butter

2 tablespoons olive oil

1 medium onion, peeled and finely
  chopped

1 medium carrot, peeled and
  finely chopped

1 stalk celery, finely chopped

100g (4oz) pancetta
  finely chopped

350g (12oz) minced beef

4 glasses red wine

300ml (½ pint) meat stock

2 tablespoons cream

1. Heat the butter and the
   olive oil in a saucepan.
2. Add the vegetables and sauté
   until golden brown. Add the
   meat and stir until browned.
3. Add half the wine and stock,
   then cover the pan and cook
   slowly, adding the remaining
   wine and stock as the liquid
   reduces and thickens.
4. After an hour, stir in the
   cream and cook uncovered
   over a medium to high heat
   until nice and thick.
5. Serve with tagliatelle.

Ragù

Bolognese meat sauce

Ragù, derived from *ragoût*, the French word for stew, is the
sauce that accompanies dishes labelled 'Bolognese'. In
Bologna it is eaten with a flat pasta such as tagliatelle –
never spaghetti.

Lasagna al forno
Baked lasagne

Lasagna is one of the oldest of all Italian dishes. The Romans called it *laganum*, probably after the pot – *lasanum* – they cooked it in. Outside Bologna, it's often served with béchamel sauce. Though pleasant enough, this is not for the purist.

For the sauce

1 medium onion, peeled and chopped

1 medium carrot, peeled and finely chopped

1 stalk celery, finely chopped

50g (2oz) bacon, finely chopped

85g (3oz) butter

115g (4oz) minced beef

115g (4oz) prosciutto, chopped

450g (1lb) tomatoes, peeled and finely chopped

4 glasses dry white wine

1. Gently sauté the vegetables with the bacon in half the butter for about 5 minutes.
2. Add the meat and stir until browned.
3. Add the tomatoes and wine, cover the pan and simmer for 1 hour.

FOR PASTA:

Follow the recipe for tortellini pasta (page 77). Divide the dough into three balls and roll them out into sheets, roughly the size of the dish in which you plan to cook the lasagne.

To make lasagne

50g (2oz) Parmesan cheese

50g (2oz) butter

1. Bring a large pot of water to the boil, and add the pasta sheets one at a time, and cook for a few seconds. Drain on kitchen paper.
2. Butter a baking dish (approximately 25 x 20cm (10 x 8in) and place a sheet of freshly cooked pasta on the bottom. Spread half of the sauce over the pasta and sprinkle it with one third of the Parmesan. Lay the second sheet of pasta over this and cover it with the remaining sauce and half the remaining Parmesan. Add the top sheet of pasta, dot with butter and sprinkle with the remaining Parmesan cheese.
3. Bake in an oven preheated to 200°C (400°F) gas mark 6 for 30 minutes.

Left: Salumeria da Bruno e Franco, probably the finest food store – and certainly the most entertaining – in Italy's food capital.

Opposite, left: Franco e Bruno's Lorenzo in flamboyant dress.

Opposite, centre: Preparing fresh spinach tagliatelle.

Opposite, right: Farfalle – butterfly shaped pasta – are made by hand in the workroom.

LA ROSSA, LA DOTTA, LA GRASSA

Bologna has its nicknames: La Rossa, the Red, due to its strong socialist tradition and commitment to progressive politics. La Dotta, the learned, because it is home to Europe's oldest university. And La Grassa, the fat, for obvious reasons, though not at street level – the industrious natives are noticeably skinny. Of course, they don't all adhere as rigorously to the Bolognese classics as Alessandra. But food takes on an importance here that is extreme even by the standards of a food-obsessed nation.

Bologna is not the most beautiful city in Italy. Its 70 kilometres of red-brick porticoes and galleries that offer shade in summer and respite in winter, give it a distinctive, strangely bulky appearance, and it has its share of striking monuments, most famously, the Due Torri, the twin towers that lean precariously at one end of Via Ugo Bassi, the city's main thoroughfare. There are fine museums such as the Pinacoteca Nazionale, which houses Titians, El Grecos, Tintorettos and the works of Bologna's lesser-known masters. But it is ultimately a working city: industrious, energetic, prosperous. But no other city I know displays food in such a beautifully evocative and seductive manner as Bologna. Its herb market is famous throughout Italy for its quality and abundance, though its remit covers cheese, bread and meat and well as fresh herbs. But it is perhaps in its famous alimentari, or specialist food shops, that the art of display reaches its zenith.

Tamburini is perhaps the most famous food store in Bologna, and is certainly the most photographed, not least because every day a monk or nun collects alms from outside its entrance. The shop stands out from the markets of Via Drapperie, and close to the central square of Piazza Maggiore, with its bulky, half-decorated cathedral. Next door is Bologna's most celebrated bakery Pasticceria Atti e Figli. But my own favourite food store in this city so rich in them is La Salumeria da Bruno e Franco on Via Oberdan, a quick stroll south from the Piazza Maggiore.

LA SALUMERIA DA BRUNO E FRANCO

'Salumeria' is a bit of a misnomer, for while there's no shortage of fine meats on display in this often frantic little shop, it also offers cheeses, fresh pasta and a remarkable array of freshly made delicacies that change daily: grilled aubergines decorated with zucchini flowers; skewers of fresh seafood; artichokes Roman-style. They also sell a mixture of salt, spices and herbs called salmoia that adds a taste of Bologna to any dish.

Panna cotta
Cream custard

Simple, dairy laden, ample and rich, the Bolognese diet is far removed from the much-lauded Mediterranean diet found elsewhere in Italy. Panna cotta concludes a Bolognese meal as it began. Panna cotta is that rare thing, a dessert that accompanies wine well – in this case, a glass of sparkling, red Lambrusco, the light wine of Emilia.

Ingredients

300ml ($^{1}/_{2}$ pint) double cream

2 tablespoons sugar

8 drops vanilla essence

1 teaspoon gelatine

2 tablespoons cold water

1. Simmer the cream with the sugar and vanilla for 2 minutes.
2. Dissolve the gelatine in 2 tablespoons of cold water and beat well into cream. Pour into 4 small individual serving bowls.
3. Chill the panna cotta until set (about 2 hours).

The shop is fronted by three men — young Lorenzo, older Arrigo, and Franco — each dressed in formal, immaculately pressed white shirts, their joyful presence emphasised by the flamboyant red hats they wear. They make every bit as much effort in the presentation of their wares as they do of themselves. Their enthusiasm is boundless. 'This is splendid.' 'This is very good.' 'The best', they say to an endless line of locals stocking up and asking what's new? what's good today? 'You want to see our laboratory?' Franco asks me, using the Italian word for what is in reality their workroom, but which conjures up images of bizarre experiments in a sterile environment. I, of course, am only too pleased to say yes.

He leads me across the road to a first floor room bustling with activity where women are rolling out the pasta dough. 'It's a beautiful smell, isn't it, like perfume,' says Franco before returning to man the shop. The women follow exactly the same process as Alessandra, sliding the cutter over the rolls of pasta, leaving tiny squares behind. But this time, they pinch each one in the middle to create farfalle, 'butterflies'. 'A simple tomato sauce will go well with it, or put it in some salad, especially when it's this hot,' I'm advised by one of the workers. Behind a machine is mixing a green mash. 'What's that?' I ask. 'That's spinach. We'll colour tagliatelle with that.' A little taste of Parma or Modena, the rivals up the road — the old Roman road of Via Emilia. I'm not sure Alessandra would approve of such treacherously un-Bolognese activity, but the attention to detail, the display of delicate craft, is typical of the food artisans of the rarely disputed capital of *la cucina Italiana*.

Above right: Selling beans in Bologna's covered herb market. The city's markets are full of hidden treasures.

Right: Bologna's distinctive galleries offer protection from bitterly cold winters and unbearably hot summers.

CHAPTER 5: TUSCANY

LAND OF PLENTY

The approach to the city of Lucca, in the north of Tuscany, is unforgettable. From the air it must look like a sun at the centre of its own universe. From the six gates of its perfectly preserved, entirely intact medieval walls bolstered by imposing bastions, radiate the roads that offer passage to the surrounding countryside, though before one samples that notable pleasure, Lucca itself is worthy of attention. The least visited of Tuscany's great renaissance centres, it has always been something of an exception. Independent from 1369 to 1847, grown rich on the silk trade, it might once have conquered Florence, but its haughty, aristocratic nature, still apparent today – and the death of its greatest soldier, Castruccio Castracani – kept it to itself.

A wealthy, conservative stronghold in left-leaning Tuscany, it is the birthplace of Giacomo Puccini, the greatest of all Italian melodists, and home to a surfeit of handsome churches, none greater than San Michele, with its gorgeous white façade topped by an archangel delicately balanced on the great loggia, like the decoration for a cake. Inside, tucked away at the right-hand end of the nave, is Filipino Lippi's radiant depiction of saints Jerome, Sebastian, Rocca and Helen; outside, locals and visitors sip coffee and lick ice cream, gazing upwards at San Michele's twisted columns, each of which is subtly distinct from the other.

Left: Caffè di Simo, on Lucca's Via Fillungo, once frequented by Lucca's favourite son, composer Giacomo Puccini.

Left: Homemade cantucci, studded with pistachios, are the traditional accompaniment to Tuscany's sweet Vin Santo wine.

Opposite: Roberto Pelagi of Fattoria Maionchi; the city of Lucca, secure behind its medieval walls; civic prosperity in Lucca's Piazza San Michele.

Above: The 'wedding cake' tiered church of San Michele, Lucca's finest.

Above, right: Products of a land of plenty on display in Lucca's busy central market.

Opposite: Horses roam the olive groves of Fattoria Colle Verde.

AT THE BOTTOM OF A BARREL

Lucca lies at the lowest point of a valley, compared by one eighteenth-century traveller to the bottom of a barrel. It's a barrel full of olive oil. For in the opinion of many, the hills surrounding Lucca produce the finest olive oil in the world. It's a unique environment, perfect for the task. Shielded from harsh north winds – the Tramonte – by the long spine of the Apennine mountains, the climate is tempered too by the mild breezes that blow in from the sea, just 30 kilometres away. Since 1560, the estate of Colle Verde, a natural amphitheatre of terraces near the village of Matraia to the east of Lucca, has been producing olive oil, and wine. Today it's the domain of Piero Tartagni, a former documentary film-maker, loosely dressed in the heat. We meet in his seventeenth-century office, a shady jumble of books, accounts and antiques that looks down on his 27 hectares of steeply banked land, three-quarters of which is planted with olive trees – the rest is vine. It once belonged to the Guinigi family, relatives of the Arnolfini famously depicted by Van Eyck, who in the sixteenth century abandoned the silk trade when it was mortally damaged by the discovery of the New World, to concentrate on the fruits of their own land. Olives have been produced here ever since.

'There was a large oil press, a communal one, in the village for years,' says Piero, 'but to be honest, it was more trouble than it was worth.' He has his own new one now, of shiny stainless steel, in a small room opposite his office, where the fruit of 3,000 plants, their fruit plucked by hand at the end of October, are 'processed', if that's not too vulgar a word. Hand-picking ensures that the olives reach the *frantoio* – or press – in the best possible state. But it's a substantial addition to the cost – as much as 70 per cent of the price of a top-quality Tuscan oil is the result of the harvest labour.

Fagiolini e limone

Green beans with olive oil and lemon

Tuscan cuisine embodies the essential virtues of Italian food. Fresh ingredients, simple combinations, and the minimum of fuss. The skill is all in the sourcing. The beans should be cooked very lightly and kept crisp. The grassy taste of good quality olive oil – Tuscan if at all possible – softens the sharpness of the citrus. Serve with grilled steak.

Ingredients

450g (1lb) green beans

3 tablespoons extra virgin olive oil

juice of 1 lemon

1. Top and tail the beans and remove any strings.
2. Bring a pan of water to the boil, the add the beans and cook for about 5 minutes or until al dente.
3. Mix the oil and lemon in a cup and pour it over the drained beans. Serve immediately.

Piero gives me a history lesson. 'Like so many things, the olive originated in the Middle East, in Mesopotamia – modern Iraq – about 6,000 years ago. Man first made use of it as a fuel for lamps. It slowly spread west to the Mediterranean, and by the last days of the Roman Empire, the whole of southern Europe had been planted. There are now 300 different kinds of olive – 240 of which are found in Italy. The relative expense of Italian olive oil, in particular that of Tuscany, is due not only to the labour costs, but also its low yield. While elsewhere an olive tree can be relied on to produce 120 kilos of fruit a year, in Tuscany it's a minuscule 7 kilos. The less fruit there is, the better the quality,' Piero claims. And he should know.

THE BEST OLIVE OIL IN ITALY

The best Tuscan olive oil is produced by the traditional three-step process: the olives are first ground into a paste that is then cold-pressed to produce a liquid from which the water and the oil are subsequently separated by decanting or, more commonly now, by centrifuge. I ask him if his modern steel *frantoio* makes a difference to the outcome. 'It makes no difference,' he asserts, 'though the debate continues. There's a lot of sentimentality around. People like those big stone mills.'

Frantoio is also the name given to the type of olive distinguished by its broad, ribbed leaves that accounts for 80 per cent of Colle Verde's cultivation. Leccino, milder in flavour, and Moraiolo share the other 20 per cent between them. The blend is important to the result. Some mills use more varieties, others fewer.

'Is it the best olive oil in Italy?' I ask. 'Depends what you want it for,' Piero replies. 'Fish is quite an important part of the diet of northern Tuscany, and it suits that. It has a very clean aroma, whereas that of the south is spicy, has more bitterness, which suits their grilled meats. The taste is different too. The best Sienese oil is bitter and peppery, whereas the Lucchese oil tastes more like artichokes, almonds and cypress leaves – and freshly cut grass, and green apples, too. It's a very good oil, rich in tannins and vitamin E, like all extra virgins.'

The term extra virgin is much misunderstood. 'To be an extra virgin olive oil,' says Piero, 'the oil must come from the first pressing, and contain less than one per cent of oleic acid, preferably as little as possible. That's why you have to pick the olives early, before they are ripe. Acidity increases with age.'

Opposite: Colle Verde's oil press.

Above: Its owner, Piero Tartagni.

Below: Vines at Colle Verde. Most Tuscan producers of oilve oil also produce wine.

Fagioli all'uccellino

Beans in tomato sauce

Tuscans are called, somewhat disparagingly, *Mangiafagoli*, or bean-eaters by other Italians, and in no other region is the use of beans so common. Yet it is strange to think that neither beans nor tomatoes, for which Tuscany is equally celebrated, were available to Italians before the sixteenth century when they reached the peninsula from the New World.

Beans were popular with the locals from the start, especially the haricot bean. A Florentine priest, Piero Valeriano, who had been presented with a sack of beans by Pope Clement VII, nurtured them and convinced Alessandro de Medici of their qualities. There was no greater propagandist for any cause in the great renaissance city.

The tomato took another couple of centuries before it caught on. The first imports to reach Italy from the New World were weedy and yellow, a long way from the deep rich pomodoro found on every Tuscan market stall today.

The literal translation of *Fagioli all'uccellino* is 'bird-like beans', a dish so called because the combination of garlic, sage and tomato is said to give the beans a gamey taste. It is the classic Tuscan bean dish, simple and hearty: the very essence of peasant ingenuity.

Ingredients

225g (8oz) cannellini beans, soaked for minimum of 12 hours

4 tablespoons olive oil

2 cloves garlic, peeled and mashed

1 teaspoon oregano

1 teaspoon sage

small tin 250g (10oz) Italian plum tomatoes, roughly chopped, or 4 fresh, overripe tomatoes, peeled, de-seeded and roughly chopped

1. Drain the beans, put them in a large saucepan and cover with water. Bring to the boil and simmer gently for about 90 minutes.

2. Heat the oil in a frying pan, and gently sauté the garlic, oregano and sage for about 3 minutes. Add the tomatoes and cook over a low heat for 10 minutes.

3. Drain the beans and add them to the sauce. Cook gently for another 5 minutes.

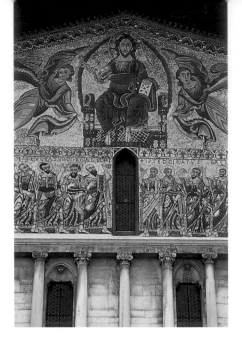

'To be an extra virgin olive oil, the oil must come from the first pressing, and contain less than one per cent of oleic acid, preferably as little as possible. That's why you have to pick the olives early, before they are ripe. Acidity increases with age.'

Piero Tartagni

GRACE AND SHARP INTELLIGENCE

Near neighbours and friends of Piero are the Maionchi-Pelagi family. Their farm – Fattoria Maionchi – sits a little further north, but in land of the same verdant splendour. The property was handed down to Pia Maria, a Maionchi woman whose family have owned the land for centuries. Her grace and sharp intelligence, especially when it comes to the subject of olive production, is clearly apparent but never demonstrative. Her daughter Elisa welcomes me to the family restaurant on a balmy Friday evening. Pictures of the greats of opera line its walls, regulars all: Pavarotti, a local boy; Renata Tebaldi, Callas's great rival; and the current darling, Angela Gheorgiou. Tom Cruise and Nicole Kidman, similarly on display, import the Maionchi oil Stateside. The food is prepared by a small army of local women using fresh ingredients, much of it the produce of the Maionchi land. Anything that is not, is still always local.

We dine outside, Elisa, her partner Lelio, a charming, funny man with a nonchalant command of culinary matters, and Roberto Pelagi, the 'Boss' as his daughter fondly calls him. Roberto, a former gynaecologist, is very ill, and painfully thin as a result.

Opposite: Conservative Lucca province is rich in both culture and agriculture.

Above: Tuscany's terraced hillsides are perfect for the production of olives and vines.

Right: The elegant leaves of the Leccino olive, grown on the slopes of Colle Verde.

ENORMOUS PRESENCE

Dressed all in black, his pale eyes shaded by ample designer glasses, Roberto Pelagi has enormous presence. His sense of taste is impeccable still. He looks askance when a bottle of his most expensive red wine is brought to the table as an accompaniment to a plate of homemade gnocchi, the beauty of which I had not experienced before, crumbly, almost all potato. It's not that he's concerned about the expense – the Maionchis are the most generous hosts imaginable – it's that the wine doesn't complement to perfection the dish we're eating. And he is a perfectionist. Roberto, with quiet authority, emphasised by the slow movement of his large, bony hands, calls for a bottle of his red DOC wine, the Colline Lucchese Rosso.

'The secret,' says Lelio, referring to the gnocchi 'is to use as much potato and as little flour as possible.' And then there are the herbs, blue, purple and green shades of rosemary, thyme and oregano plucked from Roberto's herb garden, now tended by Elisa. Combined with the DOC, it is a remarkable, supremely balanced affair, the expansive, chocolatey wine providing space for the tight components of the gnocchi to breathe. The whole experience is a perfect example of Roberto's astonishing palate. He's a man you don't meet every day.

A sort of blood sausage, follows – biroldo or San Guinago – with grapes, spices and pine nuts added. Lelio contrasts its qualities with those of a black pudding he once tasted in Scotland. 'It was a terrible experience,' he recalls with a mixture of horror and laughter. 'Boiled blood and salt.' We finish the meal with grappas and near-black cigars.

Opposite: Fattoria Maionchi's vintage olive oil press, with the *fiscoli*, mats made of coconut fibre, clearly visible.

Right: Lelio, ever elegant and nonchalant, slices into a sublime offering of Tuscan beef, served in the home of Roberto Pelagi.

Roberto talks about how he transformed the once-neglected estate into a working farm. 'In the 1950s, you know, the government was paying people to plant vines here,' he tells me with a faint smile. 'While I was still a doctor, my wife and I started to have a few tourists as guests here, and eventually we reinvented everything, producing oil and wine. We had a dream, and our expensive vice has turned into a business after 20 years. It was very interesting building it up step by step. But the food and wine was very important.' I congratulate him, his wife and their workers on the splendid food and wine.

Roberto, as an aside said: 'I've never been to a McDonalds,' a fact that didn't entirely come as a surprise. He invites me to return to their estate to see how their olive oil is produced. I accept.

HARVEST TIME

The Maionchi press, is a short, uphill walk beyond their private chapel, now, sadly, locked and stripped of its most valuable paintings due to a recent spate of robberies. There are thieves in paradise. The press employs the same three-step method as Colle Verde, but there's not much stainless steel here. The enormous millstone stands at the centre, powered by a generator. Once it was a horse that provided the power. Maria says she should use her cycling-mad son.

When the time comes along – usually the end of October – every olive is hand picked: there were 20 labourers at one point, now there are just five or six. The workers use a tiny rake called a *pettino* to pluck the olives, which they put into a *bruscola* the wicker basket each worker carries on his or her chest.

'While I was still a doctor, my wife and I started to have a few tourists as guests here, and eventually we reinvented everything, producing oil and wine. We had a dream, and our expensive vice has turned into a business after 20 years. It was very interesting building it up step by step. But the food and wine was very important.'

Roberto Pelagi

Above: Pia Maria Maionchi with the fruit from which all flows.

Above, right: Edible flowers from the Maionchi's herb garden.

Opposite: The Maionchi's three-step centrifuge separates oil from water.

I want to appreciate this wonder to the full, so Roberto shows me how to taste his olive oil. He takes one of the family's typically beautiful and valuable silver teaspoons, polishes it on the tablecloth, and adds a little of his oil. 'Let it cover all of your mouth,' he tells me as pushes his cheeks in and out, puckering his lips slowly like a goldfish. Then he starts to force it through his teeth and over his gums, hissing loudly as he does so.

After a minute and a half, maybe two, he slowly swallows the oil and picks up a piece of the dry white bread Tuscans favour. 'It should be bland. Let it soak up the oil and then you have the pure taste.' It tastes good to me, clean and mild, delicate, with no hint of the peppery pungency found in oils further south, near Florence and Siena. Roberto's verdict: 'It's good.'

So is the meal. A few cuts of mortadella – 'very underrated,' says Roberto – some spaghetti and homemade pesto, and the finest beef I have ever tasted, served almost raw, with a salad of flowers, again products of the herb garden, dressed of course in the olive oil of Fattoria Maionchi.

'It is a constant battle to produce great oil. It's us against them. We are damned by them. But it is worth it. Our oil is as low as 0.17, 0.21 in acidity, which gives it an extraordinarily full flavour. We use five different types of olive.'

Roberto Pelagi

Above: Lucca is the best preserved walled medieval city in Italy.

Above and opposite: The trappings of the Colle Verde and Maionchi wine cellars.

Bistecca alla Fiorentina
Steak Florentine style

Fine beef is available everywhere in Italy, but the classic serving is associated with the city of Florence. Always a T-bone, traditionally from the Chianina breed, the steak is grilled, *al sangue* – very rare. Dress the steak with a few lemon wedges, and serve with beans or a salad.

Ingredients

1 medium onion, peeled and coarsely chopped

1 medium carrot, peeled and coarsely chopped

1 celery stalk, coarsely chopped

4 tablespoons extra virgin olive oil

3 cloves garlic, peeled and mashed

2 tablespoons fresh, chopped rosemary

4 tomatoes, peeled and chopped

half a bottle dry white wine

1 handful coarsely chopped basil leaves

4 tablespoons Parmesan cheese, grated

4 T-bone steaks

1. Fry the onion, carrot and celery in half the oil until the onion is golden.
2. Add the garlic and the rosemary and cook for 2 minutes.
3. Add the tomatoes and the wine and simmer for 15 minutes until the sauce has thickened. Add the basil, Parmesan cheese and the remaining olive oil and stir.
4. Grill the steaks and serve with the sauce.

Castagnaccio
Chestnut cake

In Lucchesi cuisine, chestnuts are autumn favourites, pureed to accompany game, or as here, ground into flour to make savoury cakes, not desserts. The rustic flavour is typically Tuscan, and slices of the cake make a delightful appetiser dipped into the area's sweet wine, Vin Santo.

Ingredients

225g (8oz) chestnut flour

about 600ml (1 pint) water

3 tablespoons extra virgin
   olive oil

50g (2oz) pine nuts

50g (2oz) raisins, soaked and
   drained

1 teaspoon fresh chopped rosemary

1. Put the flour into a blender and add the water in a thin stream until you have a smooth batter with a fairly stiff consistency.

2. Stir in half the oil and pine nuts, all the raisins and the rosemary.

3. Pour the cake mixture into a lightly oiled rectangular cake tin about 15 x 30cm (6 x 12in).

4. Scatter the rest of the pine nuts on top, lightly drizzle with the remaining olive oil and bake in an oven preheated to 200°C (400°F) gas mark 6 for 45 minutes. Serve hot.

CHAPTER 6: PUGLIA

HARVESTING THE LAND

When, in the thirteenth century, the Holy Roman Emperor Frederick II passed through Puglia's bleak limestone escarpment, the High Murgia, on his way to the Holy Land, his men were in a terrible state, stricken by epidemic, their journey of redemption doomed as it had barely begun. The ravaged army sought shelter behind the megalithic walls of Altamura, where they recovered due, Frederick thought, to their exposure to the town's pure, dry air. Returning from the Fifth Crusade, which ended in the conquest of Jerusalem, Frederick honoured the salvation of his troops with the building of Altamura's stately, simple but imposing cathedral of Santa Maria dell'Assunta, which to this day, dominates the town's *centro storico*. Its steep steps are now the meeting place for the town's youth who gather there in the balmy summer nights to eat gelati as young families push their offspring around in a passegiata that extends till way past midnight, as is the norm in southern Italy. Meanwhile, slim, capped old men gather to play cards or watch football in the clubs of rival political parties, their offices dotted around the old centre's cramped but orderly confines. Altamura's population, young and old, is as striking in appearance as the town they are privileged to inhabit.

The pure, dry air is still celebrated, not least because of its key role in the creation of Italy's finest bread for which Altamura thoroughly deserves its title, 'Il città del pane'. It stands like a crown atop the endless horizon of golden fields of wheat. The countryside supplies the grain, the town provides the air and water.

Opposite: Bread from the ovens of Panificio Di Gesù; mingling outside one of Altamura's many social clubs; freshly milled durum wheat is delivered.

Right: Life is easy in prosperous Altamura, a city built on bread.

CITTÀ DEL PANE

Beppe di Gesù is stocky, unshaven, impassioned, full of energy, his head never still, a man concerned never to let anything slip his attention. We're taking a glass of iced tea in a cafe opposite his family's *panificio*, or bakery, just outside Altamura's walls. 'Ciao. Salve. Buongiorno.' He greets everyone here as they flit in and out; there's no lingering in the cafes of southern Italy. We discuss the creation of this book with the cafe's owner. I explain the concept, Beppe and the owner offer their comments. 'Venice, risotto? What about Milan?' 'Coffee, Turin? Don't forget Trieste too.' But there's no argument about my chapter on bread. In fact, it's barely discussed. When I tell them that I considered the bread of Tuscany as worthy of examination, the owner looks away, and Beppe laughs. 'Altamura, città del pane,' he reminds me. 'I didn't invent that.'

He did not, but his family's bakery, founded in 1838, does much to maintain Altamura's standing with panophiles, if there's such a word. When we step inside the little shop that fronts the bakery on Via Pimentei, it is packed with regulars – chomping and chatting away. The shop's walls are adorned with images of saints, with an autographed photograph of Pope John Paul II taking pride of place above the counter. Tradition speaks loudly here, like the customers. You could hardly imagine a scene more typically Italian: popes, pane and populi.

A local lawyer taking a break is happy to recount Di Gesù's virtues to me. 'Bread without equal,' he concludes between bites of focaccia – strikingly similar to a traditional, albeit thicker, type of pizza, than the lame products that bear the name focaccia outside Italy. The Di Gesù's focaccia comes in variety of styles, topped with tomato, olives, oil and oregano, potato (a carbohydrate fest!) or onion. It's the street food of Puglia; a stream of children claim it from the Di Gesù counter. It's a healthy, nutritional and filling snack that's miles away from the sweet, processed garbage beloved of the major food conglomerates, that is foisted on children elsewhere in the world.

Opposite: Pane and focaccia piled high before the ovens of Altamura's Panificio Di Gesù.

Above, left: Focaccia may be a term much used by supermarkets, but the real thing belongs to Puglia.

Left: 'Bread without equal' served by the slice in the shopfront of Di Gesù's bakery.

Above: Threshing
by hand still takes
place in Puglia.

Above, right:
Wheat arrives at
the mill for
processing.

Opposite: Durum
wheat as far as the
eye can see.

A RICH PLACE THESE DAYS

'That batch is for Piacenza, that one for Padua,' Beppe informs me, as we walk through the beaded curtain that separates shop from bakery, examining the trays of Altamuran loaves waiting to be boxed up and sent to delicatessens throughout the Italian north (they plainly prefer this stuff to the products of Tuscany, too).

I confess to surprise at the affluence and industry of Altamura, not qualities one immediately associates with the Italian south. Pasquale, Beppe's father, smiles 'It's a rich place these days,' he says. 'It's full of bankers and sports stars. Things have changed a lot over the years. Beppe is joined by his cousin, Gino, tall, masculine, muscular, a mirror image of his late father, Francesco, whose portrait hangs in the bakery office.

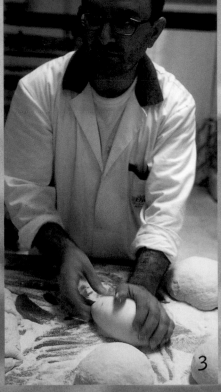

1. In Altamura, bread-making is less arduous than it was, thanks to the introduction of kneading machines, but the quality of the bread is still dependent upon the skill of the bakers.

2. After three risings, the dough is hand-kneaded.

3. The dough is shaped into the distinctive rounded style of classic Altamuran bread.

4. Pane accavallato or, in the local dialect, *u sckuanète* is the name given to the most common form of bread. Each one is individually styled by hand, and left to stand, forming its distinctive crust.

5. The pagnotta, the loaf ready for the oven, is just one of a batch of 230 loaves, baked for 75 minutes in an oven fired by hardwood.

4

5

Pane di Altamura
Altamuran bread

Like the Neapolitan pizza, the bread of Altamura is so dependent on local conditions such as the air, water and, not least, the sublime skills of the bakers, that it is impossible to recreate it exactly elsewhere. But this recipe, if followed carefully, and without skimping on the quality of ingredients, should result in a fair approximation.

Francesco's brothers, Andrea, Luca – and Pasquale – are the generation now in charge of Di Gesù, but one senses the baton being handed on, such is Beppe's energetic, hands-on role in the operation.

Beppe and Gino explain the process that turns flour, leavening, water and salt into bread. 'If you look at the bread of Altamura,' says Beppe, 'it's characterised by a thick, dark crust, which contrasts with the creamy golden yellow inside. It's because we only use durum wheat, grano duro, the stuff that's normally used to make pasta.'

Left: Pasquale, nephew Gino and son Beppe di Gesù.

Right: Going, going, gone...

For the leavening

225ml (8fl oz) warm mineral
    water

1 teaspoon dry yeast

225g (8oz) unbleached plain flour

1. Put the water in a bowl and
   sprinkle on the yeast. Leave
   for 3 minutes then stir.
2. Add the flour and stir until
   thick and gooey.
3. Leave for at least an hour
   covered with a clean, damp
   tea towel. Leave in the
   fridge overnight.

For the bread

450ml (16fl oz) warm mineral
    water

1 kilo (2lb 2oz) semolina

350ml (12fl oz) cool mineral
    water

1 teaspoon salt

extra virgin olive oil

1. Place the leavening in a
   large bowl, add the warm
   water and break up by hand.
   (It will have hardened but
   should still be moist.)
2. Add half of the semolina and
   work in until the mixture is
   thick but still viscous.
3. Cover with a clean, damp tea
   towel and leave to rise for
   3 hours or until the mixture
   is marked with bubbles.
4. A little at a time, add the
   cool water and the remaining
   semolina. Add salt and knead
   lightly in the bowl.
5. Turn the dough out onto a
   wooden board sprinkled with
   semolina. Knead for at least
   10 minutes, or until smooth.
6. Clean the bowl and brush it
   with oil. Place the dough in
   it, and cover with a damp tea
   towel. Leave for 2 hours.

TO BAKE:

1. Preheat the oven to 220°C
   (425°F) gas mark 7.
2. Flatten the dough and shape
   it into 2 rounds, each
   approximately 25cm (10in)
   in diameter.
3. Place on a baking tray and
   bake for 15 minutes, then
   reduce the oven temperature
   to 190°C (375°F) gas mark 5,
   and bake for another
   45 minutes or until the
   loaves are golden.
4. Allow to cool on a rack
   before serving.

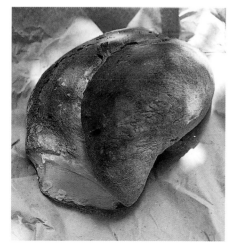
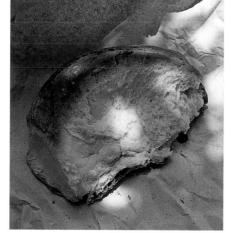

'If you look at the bread of Altamura it's characterised by a thick, dark crust, which contrasts with the creamy golden yellow inside. It's because we only use durum wheat, grano duro, the stuff that's normally used to make pasta.'

Beppe di Gesù

It's better known outside Italy as semolina, high in protein, rich in the gluten that gives the Altamuran dough its remarkable elastlclty. He shows me the bags of flour from which it's made, from the surrounding area, from Basilicata too, but mainly from the vast and arid Tavoliere plain near the city of Foggia in northern Puglia.

On the bakery's tables men are working the dough, forming the distinctive shape of the pane accavallato, the most popular style of Altamuran bread, a round base topped by a little ball, which looks a little like the flying saucers of American B movies of the 1950s. At the heart of the process is the *lievito madre*, the 'mother', the leavening that is regenerated daily by hand through the combination of water and the airborne yeasts peculiar to Altamura. The madre can be traced back to the same leavening used by Beppe's great grandfather. 'That and the flour, and the water. That's what's important,' says Beppe.

There's something antediluvian about the landscape that surrounds Altamura. Anyone who has seen Pier Paolo Pasolini's great film *The Gospel According to Saint Matthew*, which was filmed in Puglia and neighbouring Basilicata, will recognise its parched look. In a sense, antediluvian is what it is, and not just because the remains of numerous dinosaurs, from 70 million years ago, were discovered in the surroundings as recently as the late 1990s.

Melanzane ripiene al forno
Aubergine stuffed with olives, tomatoes and capers

Aubergines are used widely in Puglian cuisine and throughout southern Italy. The Italian melanzana looks nothing like the darker aubergine of the Middle East, but these can be used in the recipe instead. In Sicily, grilled, aubergines often accompany spaghetti.

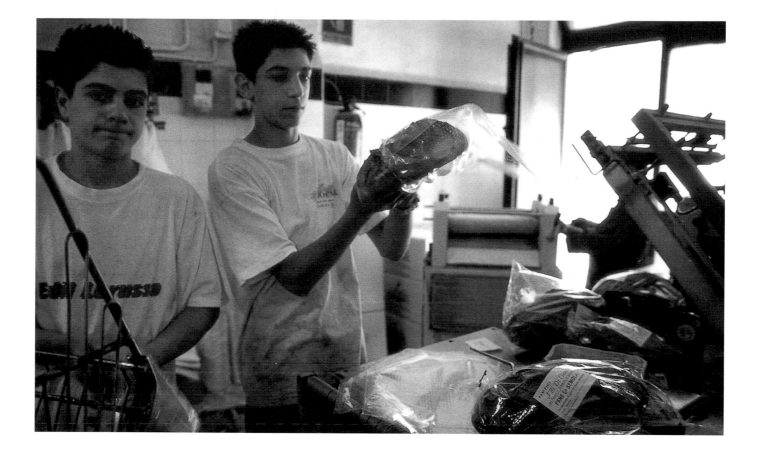

Ingredients

4 medium aubergines

salt

6 tablespoons extra virgin
  olive oil

100g (4oz) breadcrumbs

30 black olives, chopped

8 ripe tomatoes, peeled and
  chopped

1 tablespoon capers, drained and
  chopped,

2 garlic cloves, peeled and
  crushed

1 tablespoon chopped basil

90g (3oz) grated Pecorino cheese

1. Cut the aubergines in half lengthways.
   Sprinkle with plenty of salt and set aside
   for at least 1 hour. Rinse and dry.

2. Cut out the insides of each aubergine half,
   leaving 5mm (½ in) of flesh around the skin.

3. Chop the flesh and set aside in a small bowl.

4. Heat the oil in a large frying pan, brown the
   aubergine halves and drain on kitchen paper.

5. Mix the chopped aubergine with the remaining
   ingredients, plus a dash of olive oil.

6. Fill the aubergine halves equally, place them
   in a roasting tin and bake in a preheated
   oven at 220°C (425°F) gas mark 7 for 1 hour.
   Serve immediately.

Above: Altamura
is home to
numerous bakeries.
As the bakeries are
family affairs,
children often turn
up to help out after
their school day.

There's very little water, the land is denied refreshment, and its relative fruitfulness is down to the hard work of its farmers, who work wonders to make Puglia the largest source of vine and olive in all Italy. But where does the water come from, I ask Beppe, reminding him of the description of this land penned by the Roman writer Horace, 'Apulia siticulosa,' 'thirsty Puglia'. 'The rock here is made of calcium, so it's very porous. Therefore there's very little reserve of water. But we have an aqueduct that transports water here from Naples. The water you drink here is Neapolitan.' The water that benefits the pizzaioli of Naples, comes to the aid of the bakers of Altamura, too.

In the corner of the bakery sits a modern kneading machine, with arms like a cradling mother perpetually dropping her child, where the dough is produced from one part leavening to five parts durum wheat and a lot of water. Once the kneading is over, the dough is covered with a cotton cloth to ensure that it rises evenly. After an hour and a half of standing, sometimes more, the dough is shaped by hand into the traditional Altamuran shape, and left to stand for half an hour as its distinctive crust forms. It's then shaped again, left to stand for 15 minutes or so, and the loaf, the pagnotta, is ready for the oven.

There are three ovens in the bakery, but pride of place goes to the large wood-burning oven that's changed little in a century. 'Women used to bring in their own loaves to bake here. It was like a communal oven for the town,' Beppe recalls, 'but that doesn't really happen anymore.' In the past, the baker marked the initials of the head of the family on the loaves with a wooden or iron stamp before putting them in the oven.

The oven looks much the same shape as those of the pizzerias of Naples, bricked up, and with a stone baking surface made of mazzero, a particular type of stone that can tolerate the 350°C (660°F) at which the bread is baked. The fuel is hardwood, such as oak, fired every morning to an intense heat, the ashes swept away, and the loaves placed inside, filling every available space. They stay there for about 75 minutes. In a single session, 230 loaves will be made. The same process carries on every day, until the week's production ends on Saturday evening. It begins again at 5pm every Sunday when the madre is regenerated once more. On and on, the process never ceases.

'The rock here is made of calcium, so it's very porous. Therefore there's very little reserve of water. But we have an aqueduct that transports water here from Naples. The water you drink here is Neapolitan.'

Beppe di Gesù

Above: A batch of loaves leave Di Gesù's old oven.

Right: Kneaded dough is covered with a cotton cloth to ensure that it rises evenly.

Far right: Dough awaits the attention of the bakers.

Tiella di Puglia

Mussels, potatoes and courgette casserole

As one reaches the long coastline of Puglia, seafood becomes a common ingredient, especially the region's delicious mussels. Puglia is unusual among Italian regions in making much of the potato – it often surprises visitors to Italy how little the locals make of what is a staple elsewhere. Courgettes here are – like most Italian vegetables – excellent. The very different textures of the ingredients combine to marvellous effect.

Ingredients

1kg (2lb 3oz) cleaned mussels

30ml (1fl oz) water or white wine

450g (1lb) small potatoes

225g (8oz) small courgettes

225g (8oz) red onions, finely sliced

grated Pecorino cheese

3 tablespoons oregano

1. Place the mussels in a pan with the water or wine, cover and heat gently until the mussels open.
2. Discard any unopened mussels, remove from their shells and drain. (Leave a few in their shells to use as a garnish.)
3. Thinly slice the potatoes, and cut the courgettes into long strips.
4. Lightly oil a casserole dish and layer it with half of the potatoes, courgettes, onions, Pecorino, oregano and mussels. Repeat with the remaining ingredients. Cover with foil and bake at 200°C (400°F) gas mark 6 for 30 minutes. Remove the foil and bake for 30 minutes more.

Pollo arrosto
Puglian roast chicken

Puglia is now economically the most successful of southern Italian regions, grown rich on its abundance of wine and oil. But its cuisine reflects its less affluent past, hence the love of feast dishes such as this one, embraced especially during Easter festivities

Ingredients

1 1.6kg (3lb 8oz) chicken with giblets

2 tablespoons extra virgin olive oil

1 small onion, peeled and finely chopped

2 garlic cloves, peeled and finely sliced

50g (2oz) breadcrumbs

1 teaspoon chopped capers

2 tablespoons oregano

1 tablespoon Pecorino cheese

1 medium egg

225ml (8fl oz) white wine

1. Preheat the oven to 200°C (400°F) gas mark 6.
2. Finely chop the chicken liver and heart. Heat the oil in a small pan and sauté the giblets until browned.
3. Place the giblets in a small bowl with the onion, garlic, breadcrumbs, capers, oregano and Pecorino cheese.
4. Add the egg to the mixture, which should be firm but still moist.
5. Stuff the chicken with the mixture and rub a little olive oil into the skin.
6. Place the chicken in a roasting tray and cook for 45 minutes. Baste with the wine. Reduce the temperature to 175°C (350°F) gas mark 4 and cook for a further 45 minutes. Baste with pan juices every 10 to 15 minutes. Allow the chicken to stand before serving.

'The bread of Altamura lasts much longer than other breads. Shepherds could spend a week or two in the mountains with nothing but bread and water, and maybe a little oil and salt. This is no ordinary bread.'

Beppe di Gesù

STAFF OF LIFE

The traditional Puglian loaf comes in three different sizes: ½ kilo, 1 kilo and 5 kilos. They lie freshly baked, on the *tavolo*, the long wooden boards that would once have been carried precariously through the town by *garzone*, boys on bikes. 'Bread really was the staff of life in the past,' says Beppe. 'Families would eat as much as 25 kilos of bread each week. Now that's down to three and a half. It's still very important to eat bread,' he stresses as he feeds me a list of its nutritional benefits. 'Bread should be a major part of the 2,000 calories each of us need every day.'

'The bread of Altamura lasts much longer than other breads,' Beppe informs me. 'Shepherds could spend a week or two in the mountains with nothing but bread and water, and maybe a little oil and salt. Even to our refined tastes, the bread of Altamura holds its freshness for two or three days longer than ordinary bread. This is no ordinary bread.'

Horace, though fearful of Puglia's arid climate, was the first publicly to praise Altamura's bread. 'Far the best bread to be had,' he wrote in his *Satires*, 'so good that the wise traveller takes a supply of it for his onward journey.' Two millennia on, it's hard to disagree.

Walking around Altamura, one notices that bakeries abound. Even the newsagents display the edition of the magazine *Ergo*, which celebrated the Altamura bakers' award of a DOP, Denominazione de Origine Protetta, the European Union's recognition of their distinctive creations, and their commitment to its protection. It's not just a question of quality, though one taste of the pane or focaccio puts an end to that particular argument, but quantity too. And age. One bakery, the Forno di Santa Chiara, an alley's length from the cathedral in Via Ciccarella, dates back to 1423 and remains in operation today.

Opposite: Pasquale holds the *lievito madre*, the 'mother' leavening.

Left: Decorative loaves at San Chiara, Altamura's oldest surviving bakery.

Below: Pane de capriccio, served to celebrate the birth of a child.

Torta di ricotta

Ricotta cake

Made of sheep's milk, ricotta features strongly in the
cuisine of the South, and is often used as an addition to
dishes in the manner of Parmesan. It comes in many forms:
salted and unsalted, fresh and dried. Use salted, fresh
ricotta for this dish, which is enlivened by the addition of
grappa, a sometimes harsh liqueur made from grape skins.

Ingredients

450g (1lb) ricotta cheese

4 medium eggs, separated

3 tablespoons flour

225g (8oz) sugar

1 teaspoon ground cinnamon

rind of 2 medium lemons

4 tablespoons grappa

brown sugar

1. Preheat the oven to 190°C
   (375°F) gas mark 5.
2. Mix the ricotta with the
   yolks of the eggs.
3. Add the flour, sugar,
   cinnamon, lemon rind and
   grappa and stir well.
4. Beat the egg whites until
   stiff and fold them into the
   mixture. Pour into a
   buttered cake tin, 25cm
   (10in) in diameter.
5. Bake for 40 minutes.
   Sprinkle the brown sugar
   on top and serve.

HOW CAN IT COMPARE?

The Atkins Diet, the low carbohydrate fad beloved of
Hollywood stars and their entranced followers, crops up in a
couple of conversations, to be dismissed with a shrug. 'You
find me a fat person here,' says Giuseppe, Beppe's lively
younger cousin, and he has a point. But it's hardly just the
bread that accounts for the locals' slimline profiles. Pugliese
cuisine is the very epitome of the Mediterranean diet still
espoused by a majority of nutritionists, of which bread is just
a part, but an important one.

A glass of wine, grilled fish, vegetables, a little cheese and
fruit. It's the same spread that's rustled up for me in the
cool confines of a local trattoria that's a favourite of the Di
Gesù. The place is packed out at lunchtime with an almost
exclusively male clientele. The food served up would be
special elsewhere, but is taken for granted here. Elton John
can barely be heard over the room's speakers. I tell Beppe
that I have never been in a settlement of any size in Italy
where I haven't heard Elton's voice at some point or other.
'Sorry Seems to Be the Hardest Word', he sings. There's
nothing apologetic about the attitude of the Pugliese. When
we return, I'm harangued by Andrea Di Gesù for even daring
to suggest that maybe Tuscany has what many would
consider to be Italy's classic cuisine. 'La cucina Pugliese is
the best in Italy,' he asserts. 'That Tuscan bread? There's no
salt for a start. No taste. How can it compare to ours?'

Left: Altamura's
impressive duomo,
built by Holy
Roman Emperor,
Frederick II.

Centre: Caffè
Ronchi, where
Altamurans break
their evening
passegiata for an
ice cream.

Below: The loaves
of Altamura are
now recognised as a
unique product.

CHAPTER 7: NAPLES

SIMPLE PLEASURES

The historic centre of Naples, the seething, sprawling capital of the Italian South, is a tight, dimly lit warren of medieval streets, seemingly untouched by the sun – though not the heat – that lights the city's glorious bay, just a few hundred yards away but which may as well be another planet. Spaccanapoli, literally 'split Naples', the name long given to the *centro storico*, that traces the street patterns of Roman *Neapolis*, may not be the most salubrious part of this multi-faceted, ancient settlement, but it is its heart.

Here, romance cuts through the chaos. Vespas ridden by families of three or even four, really do tear down alleys bridged by lines of washing, just like in the postcards, though the *scugnizzi*, Naples' legendary street urchins, are better nourished these days, cleaner and less likely to pick the pockets or grab the bags of tourists distracted by another detail of another church.

Opposite: Da Michele's Luigi Condurro: the 'Maradona of the pizza'; Neapolitan youth, astride their Vespas; a classic pizza Margherita; boys playing football, Naples's 'other religion', in one of the city's baroque piazzas.

Above, left: Street food is a Ncapolitan staple, especially in the backstreets of the Spanish quarter.

Above: *Pizzaioli* in classic uniform of white T-shirt and cap, prepare for lunchtime at Pizzeria di Matteo.

Left: The sprawling metropolis of Naples, Italy's most compelling city.

Below, left: Vespas, ready to deliver pizzas.

Below, centre: The brooding bulk of Vesuvius faces the city from across its wide bay.

Below: Freshly cooked pizzas, oozing oil and tomato, are a favourite of the city's children.

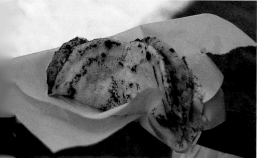

Naples' affluent classes prefer to spread out among the wide and fashionable shopping streets of Chiara, before ascending high to their homes in the hills of Vomerò on the cable cars celebrated in the song *Funiculì, funiculà*, to look down on the marvellous vista of the bay, crowned by the threatening hulk of the volcano, Vesuvius. But the modern visitor who spurns Spaccanapoli – or, as the Romans called it, *decumanus inferior* – also spurns the experience of the most vibrant living link Europe has to the medieval world. And they miss out too on the greatest of all Neapolitan creations, the pizza. It may have conquered the world, but the streets of Spaccanapoli are where the pizza was born, and it is only here that this most simple and satisfying of dishes can be found at its best.

CLASSIC COMPOSITION

Di Matteo, at the western end of Via Tribunali, is a classic Spaccanapoli pizzeria, with its front open to the street, a plain, tiled, white interior, and wood-fired *forno*, around which cluster an ensemble of pizza makers – the *pizzaioli* – dressed in their standard uniform of white T-shirt emblazoned with the name of their establishment. The outfit is often enhanced by a cap, worn at a cocked angle, more for style, one imagines, than for any purpose of hygiene. The ground floor is cramped and busy, packed with diners. The room the *pizzaioli* have to work in is minimal indeed, and the little they have is competed for with passing schoolchildren grabbing the deep-fried filled pizzas – known as calzone, 'trouser legs' elsewhere in Italy – whose rich filling of ricotta, ham and tomato, spills out on the pavement outside where the children wolf them down. Upstairs is a relative oasis of calm: eight tables spread out within a marbled interior split into three: a family group, marshalled by severe Italian women spreads over one; young lovers share another as, strangely, they examine X-rays of their teeth.

The array of pizzas served up by Di Matteo is wide for a traditional Neapolitan pizzeria, though most, on further examination, are just variations on the Margherita – the classic composition of tomato, mozzarella and basil – that conjures up the colours of the Italian flag and is named after the wife of Italy's King Umberto I. In 1889, so the story goes, the *pizzaiolo*, Raffaele Esposito was summoned to the royal residence in the hills of Capodimonte, where he presented three different pizzas to Queen Margherita. She declared the tricolore her favourite. Esposito's claim that he was the originator of the tricolore was hotly disputed, but his family's pizzeria, Brandi, at the back of the San Carlo opera house, still makes play of the fact – and good pizza – but their establishment, now something of a tourist trap, is grand by the standards of Spaccanapoli, and pizza is not an aristocratic dish.

Pizza

MAKES 4 PIZZAS, ABOUT 25CM (10IN) IN DIAMETER

Short of installing your own wood-fired oven, you cannot
possibly recreate the smokey, unctuous tang of the Neapolitan
pizza. But this recipe offers an acceptable approximation.

For the dough

1 sachet dried yeast

450g (1lb) strong white flour

1 teaspoon salt

350ml (12fl oz) warm water

1. Mix the dry ingredients
   together in a bowl, then
   stir in the warm water.
2. Make the dough into a ball
   and place it on a lightly
   floured surface. Knead
   repeatedly, turning the
   dough in on itself, then
   pushing it away from you
   with the heel of your hand.
   Continue kneading for about
   10 minutes. Add a little
   flour to stop the dough
   sticking to the board. When
   finished, the dough should
   be smooth, slightly damp on
   the surface and elastic.

A LIVING GUARANTEE

The Margherita serves as the model for a million pizzerias around the globe, but
it is only one half of the classic pairing of Neapolitan pizza. The marinara, the
other half of this celebrated duo, conjures up images of a pizza laden with
prawns, tuna and other seafood. But the marinara is the simplest of all pizzas,
topped only with tomato, garlic, oil and oregano, and the closest we have to the
pizza's Roman root, the herb-encrusted piece of stone-baked dough they called a
laganum. This most traditional of pizzas is best enjoyed in Naples' most
traditional pizzeria. Da Michele, so special it doesn't even bother to belong to
the estimable Vera Pizza Napoletana, the guild of pizzerias that combine to
guarantee the quality and tradition of Naples's archetypal dish. Da Michele, in
itself, is a living guarantee of quality and tradition.

3. Dust the dough lightly over with flour. Place in a bowl covered with a clean tea towel. Allow to rise for about 1 hour, until it nearly doubles in size.

TO PREPARE THE PIZZA:

1. Preheat the oven to 240°C (475°F) gas mark 9.
2. Flatten the dough and divide it into 4 balls.
3. Flatten each of the balls of dough into a circle. On another floured surface, rotate the circle, flattening its centre with the heel of your hand. When a ridge appears on the outside of the disk, hold the dough up with both hands letting the weight of the dough stretch the circle.

4. Spread the dough on a baking sheet dusted in flour and add your chosen topping, layering the ingredients one by one and sprinkling on the olive oil last. Bake for 8 to 10 minutes until the outer crust is brown.

TOPPINGS:

These are the classic toppings: Da Michele, the most authentic of Neapolitan pizzerias serves only these. But there are many variants, and most Neapolitan pizzerias offer a wider array. One speciality of Di Matteo's is the Pizza Bianchi, which is devoid of tomatoes, but topped with varieties of cheese, including Pecorino, Parmesan, fior di latte, and even buffalo mozzarella.

For a pizza alla marinara

3 tinned plum tomatoes, drained finely chopped

½ teaspoon minced garlic

½ teaspoon dried oregano

1 tablespoon vegetable oil

For a pizza Margherita

3 tinned plum tomatoes, drained and finely chopped

½ teaspoon finely minced garlic

15g (½ oz) fior di latte

30g (1oz) grated Pecorino

3 or 4 leaves of basil, roughly torn

1 tablespoon vegetable oil

Left: A freshly composed Margherita enters the *forno* of Da Michele's pizzeria.

Right: A calzone being prepared at Di Matteo.

NOT A PLACE TO GET LOST

Da Michele has operated from its site on Via Cesare Sersale since the 1930s, before that, from its birth in 1870, it stood across the road. It's an insalubrious part of town, choked from all sides by the traffic that streams to and from Corso Umberto, the manic thoroughfare that leads to Piazza Garibaldi, home of the city's infamous train station and many people's first, often damning sight of inner-city Naples. A more picturesque approach is to come via the narrow back alleys off Via Tribunali – but it's easy to get lost, and this is not a place to get lost, not at night anyway. If you're feeling confident, take the right turning after the church of Pio Monte della Misericordia – where hangs Caravaggio's exquisite *Seven Acts of Mercy*. Cross a couple of streets at the end of the alley – a banner hangs over one, declaring 'Only Christ can deliver peace' – and a vertical sign appears reading 'Antica Pizzeria'. That's Da Michele. Outside, on my penultimate visit, an Alsatian dog was toying with a dying pigeon. It's that kind of area, but nothing should put you off venturing there.

'You want a marinara, you have a marinara. Margheritas used to outsell marinaras. Now I'm not so sure, must be the women watching their weight, and the men their hearts.'

Luigi Condurro

Luigi Condurro, thin, tall, with a faint smile always on the edge of his lips, is now the head of this greatest of all pizza-making dynasties. Da Michele was founded by his grandfather – the eponymous Michele – whose sepia portrait hangs above the cash register, now manned by another Condurro, Sergio, Luigi's nephew. Luigi's father, Salvatore, inherited the firm and passed it on to his son. It's just after 11am, a little before the daily rush that envelops Da Michele on every day but the Sabbath, ritually observed in a staunchly Catholic city, and a few days of holiday in August. A family friend sits eating a pizza Margherita; I wonder how many he has eaten in his long life.

Opposite: The tiny kitchen at pizzeria Di Matteo.

Above: Delivering the ingredients to Da Michele.

Right: The interior of Da Michele, a Neapolitan classic.

1. Da Michele's master *pizzaiolo*, Luigi Condurro offers a masterclass in pizza-making in his very public kitchen.

2. Luigi's marble table – in full view of his customers – is as much an attraction as his pizza. Note the agliara oil container.

3. Luigi kneads the ball of pre-prepared dough, forming a near-transparent circle that's the pizza's foundation.

4. A thin layer of tomato paste is spread onto the pizza base.

5. Fior di latte is added to create a Margherita. The marinara would have received only a handful of garlic and oregano.

All the tables are marble, and most in the simple but elegant room that opens out on to the street, communal. The white walls are mirrored on either side by adverts from the 1930s advertising Peroni beer, the only alcohol served, and then in a paper cup. Beyond, centre-stage, stands the vintage *forno*, the wood-fired oven, shaped like a church bell. The wood and shavings seep out of its bricked bottom as they burn, adding to the heat of a stifling Neapolitan day. The pizzas are placed on a stone mantle as they cook, visible to all. The process of firing the oven begins anew daily, the task of two striking, imposing, but friendly young *pizzaioli*, Bruno and Emanuele. In a cool, light room to the side, batches of dough, one lot for lunchtime, another for the evening, are made using '00' flour (a refined durum wheat flour that is high in gluten) mixed in a baker's traditional *impastatrice*, and left to rise.

THE HIGHEST PRAISE

'We are the one true dynasty of Italian pizza,' says Sergio, in all modesty, 'and he's its Maradona – but he's not as crazy.' He's just paid Luigi the highest compliment any Neapolitan can receive, to be compared to the barrel-shaped Argentinian footballing genius who brought two Italian league titles and a European Cup to previously benighted Napoli. A picture of a visiting Maradona – always referred to in Naples by the beatific epithet 'Diego Armando Maradona' – hangs alongside images of the founders. Luigi is entirely deserving of such praise.

'Here's how to make a pizza,' he says, encouraging me over to the raised marble counter before the full flood of customers arrives. On the counter stands the paraphernalia of the *pizzaiolo*. Little metal bowls of raw ingredients, and a can resembling Aladdin's lamp – the *agliara* – containing a rather bland vegetable oil, never extra virgin olive oil – Luigi claims it would overpower the other flavours – from which Da Michele's masterpieces are constructed. Foodies might be flummoxed, but that's the way it is.

Above: A regular customer savours one of Da Michele's pizza Margheritas.

Right: Da Michele's vintage mirrors advertise the pizza's traditional accompaniment: Italian beer.

Spaghetti alle vongole
Spaghetti with clams

It's not all pizza in Naples. This richly
inventive city is also the home of
spaghetti, southern Italy's classic pasta
style: hard and made of durum wheat, unlike
the fresh 'eggy' style preferred in the
north of Italy. As befits a city with one of
Europe's greatest bays, seafood often
accompanies spaghetti. Usually it's the
delicate clams that live in buckets outside
many of the city's trattorias. A little
chopped hot pepper adds spice to the dish.

Ingredients

2 tablespoons extra virgin olive oil

2 garlic cloves, peeled and crushed

1.8kg (4lb) fresh clams, well cleaned

1 small, hot, red or green pepper, finely chopped

200g (7oz) dried spaghetti (as a starter)

1 handful parsley, finely chopped

1. Heat the oil and garlic in a pan large enough
   to hold the clams. Add the clams and the
   pepper. Cover and cook until the clams open,
   shaking the pan from time to time.
2. Place the clams in a bowl and keep warm. Keep
   the clam juice in the pan.
3. In the meantime, cook the spaghetti for about
   5 minutes or until al dente.
4. Drain the pasta and add it to the pan with
   the clam juices. Add the chopped parsley and
   toss until the pasta is evenly covered.
5. Divide the spaghetti into 4 bowls and top
   with the clams in their shells.

A MASTER AT WORK

Luigi picks up a pagnotte, the ball of pre-prepared dough that forms the basis of each pizza, and flattens it on the counter, rolls it around, works it, twists it, spins it. By the time he's finished, about 90 seconds later, it's an elastic width of Luigi's large, splayed hand as it hits the deck of the counter.

A thin, almost meagre layer of chopped tomato is spooned on top. The tomatoes, which taste better in Naples than perhaps anywhere else on earth, are from San Marzano, a village on the slopes of Vesuvius, reddened by the sun and made pungent by volcanic soil, salty without extra addition.

Next comes mozzarella cheese, though not the highly prized and priced mozzarella di bufala for which Campania is famous, but the less rich, less fatty fior di latte, made from cow's milk, which doesn't ooze and run when cooked. This may come as yet another surprise to the fully paid up foodie, but there can be no arguments here. The debate ended long ago. A little Pecorino Romana is added too, lending a Parmesan-like tang to the mixture. Finally, two or three whole basil leaves are plonked on top, before the whole thing is smothered in oil. Emanuele brings the *legna di forno* over. Its metal board is shaped like a little guitar.

Below: There's barely a food stall in the city that doesn't provide some variant of pizza.

Below, right: Fresh from the *forno*, a Margherita from Di Matteo.

Pollo cacciatore

Hunter's chicken

Naples is Italy's most intense urban experience, but the region of which it is the capital, Campania, is as rich in agriculture as its name - meaning countryside - suggests. Meat, a rarity in Naples, is a little more common there, but chicken predominates. This dish makes excellent use of the regions best ingredients: garlic, oil, tomatoes and wine. Use tinned tomatoes, as many of those found in supermarkets are from Campania, and have the deep, rich taste that only long exposure to the Mediterranean sun guarantees.

Ingredients

2 tablespoons extra virgin olive oil

4 chicken thighs

1 small onion, finely chopped

3 cloves garlic, finely chopped

sprig of fresh rosemary

half a glass of dry white wine

600ml (1 pint) tinned plum tomatoes

1. Heat the oil in a large pan. Turn the chickn so that it browns on all sides.
2. Add the onion, garlic and rosemary and sauté until the onions are tender.
3. Add the wine and bring the mixture to the boil.
4. Reduce the heat and add the tomatoes. Cover and allow to simmer gently for about 30 minutes.
5. Remove the chicken, then increase the heat for 2 minutes to reduce and thicken the sauce.
6. Pour the sauce over the chicken when you serve it.

Broccoli Napoletana

Neapolitan broccoli

Of all Italy's regional cuisines it is that of Naples that most embodies the much-lauded virtues of the 'Mediterranean diet'. Broccoli, among the most nutritious of all vegetables and highly regarded for its protective qualities, is the traditional food of the Neapolitan poor. This is a wonderfully tasty way to serve broccoli to children.

Ingredients

450g (1lb) head of broccoli
3 tablespoons extra virgin olive oil
3 anchovy fillets
2 garlic cloves, peeled and crushed

1. Trim the broccoli into florets, and cook in boiling water for 5 minutes. Drain.
2. In a large pan, heat the olive oil, then add the anchovies and stir until 'melted' into the oil.
3. Add the broccoli and cook uncovered over a medium heat for 10 minutes, adding the garlic halfway though. Stir until the broccoli is soft but not falling apart.

Opposite: Washing crosses the alleys of the *centro storico*.

Above: It's worth waiting for a table at Da Michele.

Luigi places the pizza on it, stretching its sides as far as possible to create the *cornicione*, the puffed up circumference that distinguishes the otherwise crisp and thin Neapolitan pizza. It goes straight into the oven. Two minutes is all it takes. 'Allora,' says Luigi. 'A Margherita. Do you want one?'

It seems churlish to refuse a creation of Naples' most revered *pizzaiolo*, but the first time I ever came to Da Michele, 20 years ago or so, I ordered and subsequently devoured a marinara, not knowing what I would receive. That moment remains one of the two or three greatest taste experiences of my life. I explain this to Luigi, by way of turning down his generous offer of a Margherita. He laughs, looks proud, and pats me on the back. 'You want a marinara, you have a marinara. Margheritas used to outsell marinaras. Now I'm not so sure,' says Luigi. 'Must be the women watching their weight, and the men their hearts.' Again he takes the pagnotte, twists and turns it, and adds the tomato. But now he takes three very thickly sliced pieces of garlic, and a handful of oregano, plus the oil. Two minutes later, it's delivered to me.

Sfogliatelle
Breakfast pastry folds

Breakfast in Napoli is a rushed, frenetic affair, sometimes little more than a sugary thimble of espresso, but usually accompanied by the sfogliatelle that are regarded by the rest of Italy as quintessentially Neapolitan. It's hardly the healthy, substantial breakfast recommended by modern nutritionists but, given that the rest of the Neapolitan diet is so healthy, it can be forgiven. Sfogliatelle are actually quite difficult to make, so this recipe requires careful attention. Sfogliatelle also make a delicious dessert, especially when accoompanied with Marsala wine.

For the dough

425g (15oz) plain flour

175ml (6fl oz) warm water

1. Mix the flour and water together in a bowl to form.
2. Knead the dough on a floured surface. Cover and chill in the fridge for 2 hours.

For the filling

225ml (8fl oz) water

100g (4oz) sugar

100g (4oz) semolina

250g (10oz) ricotta

2 egg yolks

2 teaspoons vanilla extract

¼ teaspoon cinnamon

10g (½ oz) candied orange peel

50g (2oz) melted butter

Left: The looming hulk of Vesuvius is the spectacular backdrop to the bay of Naples.

At Euro 3.10, it's easily the best-value gourmet experience in Europe, fit for a Bourbon king, especially with a beer. How many pizzas are made on the planet daily? What are the odds a great one? At Da Michele, it's a racing certainty.

The following day, I return, for another marinara. It's the usual heave of locals, but on the table next to me are two Americans, Bob and Sue, who run a string of Italian restaurants in Seattle. 'We're on a cruise,' says Bob, 'and we're only in Naples for a few hours, but we had to come here, it's a legend.'
I congratulate them on their choice. They're not disappointed. Bob's plate is empty by the time my marinara, as delicious as ever, arrives. Da Michele is their only stop in a city brimful of attractions, packed with art, crammed with outstanding religious buildings, remarkable classical ruins, a street life unequalled elsewhere in Europe, and the continent's finest bay. But Bob and Sue have it right. If there's one thing to do, just one place to visit when in Naples, it's Da Michele.

1. Put the water and sugar in a pan and bring to the boil.
2. Sift the semolina into the boiling water. Lower the heat and cook until thick.
3. Purée the ricotta in a food processor. Add to the semolina mixture and cook for about 8 minutes, stirring constantly.
4. Remove from the heat and stir in the egg yolks, vanilla extract, cinnamon and orange peel.
5. Place in a shallow bowl, cover and chill until set.

TO MAKE THE SFOGLIATELLE:

1. Divide the dough into two balls, and roll out each on a floured board to a size of 30 x 50cm (12 x 20in).
2. Cut each piece of dough in half lengthways to create 4 strips of dough each 15 x 25cm (6 x 10in).
3. Glaze one strip with butter and roll it into a tight cylinder from a short end.
4. Glaze a second strip of dough. Position one end on top of the end of the first strip. Continue to roll, adding the third and fourth strips. Wrap in plastic and chill overnight until firm.
5. Remove the plastic and slice the roll into 12 equal pieces. (Each piece should resemble tagliatelle).
6. Take one slice of dough and flatten it out with the heel of your hand on a floured board, forming an oval shape about 19cm (7½ in) long.
7. Put a large dessertspoon of the filling onto one half of each oval, then fold the dough over the filling, pinching the edges together.
8. Arrange each sfogliatella on a lightly oiled baking tray and bake in the oven at 200°C (400°F) gas mark 6 for 25 minutes.

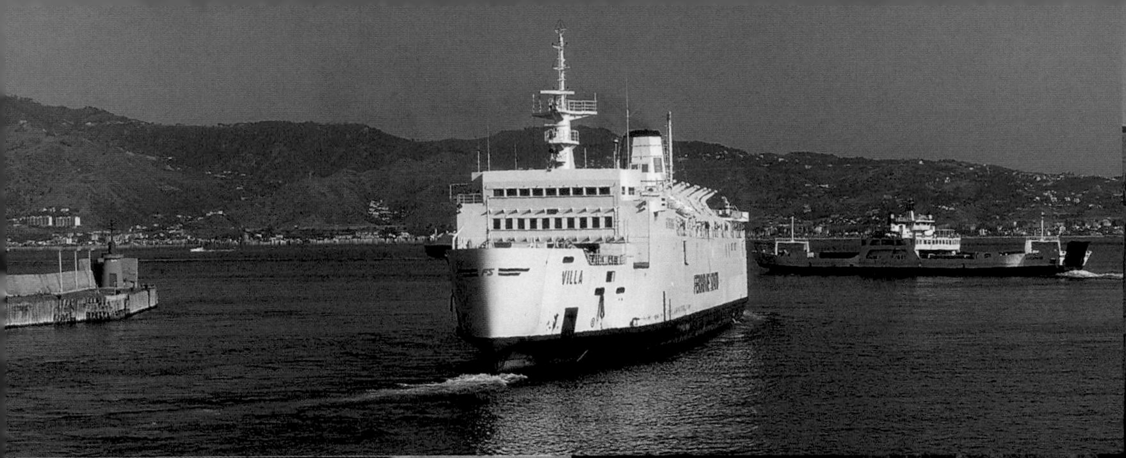

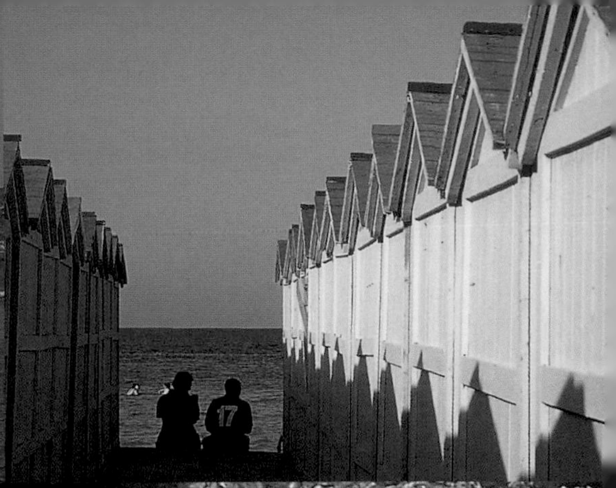
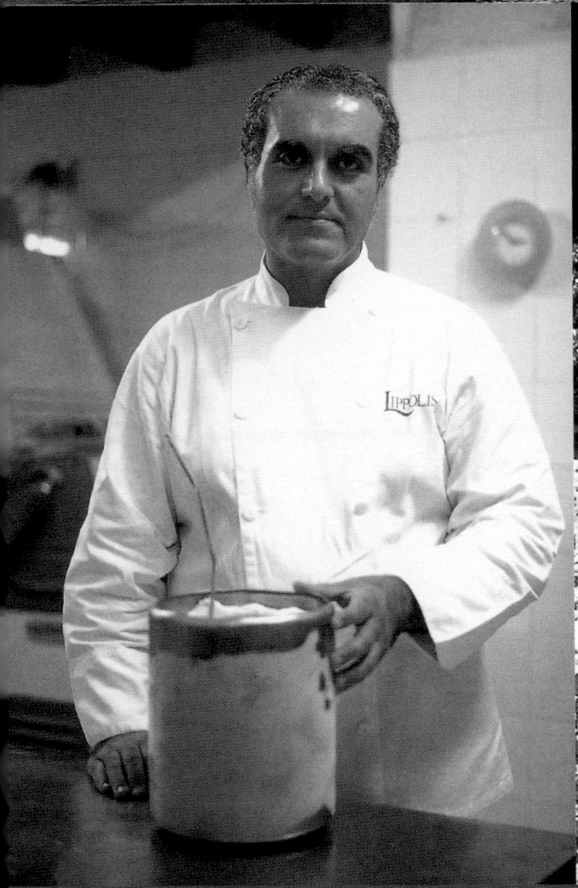

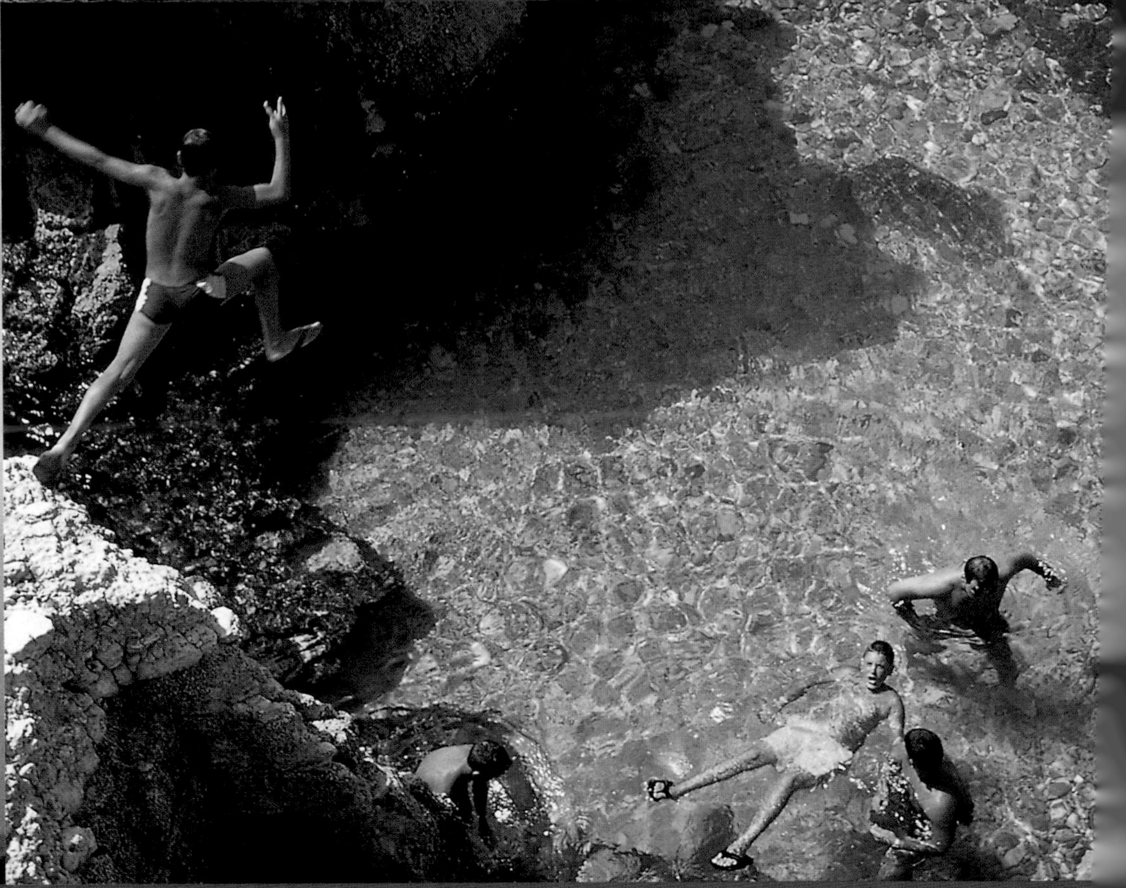

CHAPTER 8: SICILY

SWEET, SUNLIT ISLAND

Opposite: Tino di Bartolomeo prepares granità; the ferry makes its way across the Straits of Messina; between beach huts and the sea; boys jump into Syracuse's cooling harbour.

Above, left: Fishing boats: harvesters of Sicily's three seas.

Above: Granità, 'buttered' on a brioche, is the traditional Syracuse sweet breakfast.

Ortygia, the oldest part of the ancient Sicilian city of Syracuse, was the Greeks' Manhattan: a small, densely populated, immensely creative peninsula jutting out into the Ionian Sea. It was the birthplace of the great Greek mathematician and physicist Archimedes; the playwright Aeschylus visited, as did the philosopher Plato, as advisor to the Syracusan king Dionysius. Thucydides, historian of the Greeks' many military adventures, regarded the Syracusan rebuttal of Athens' great fleet in 415BC as the greatest of all military victories. Under Roman rule, Cicero, the greatest orator of the ancient world, was its governor, and Saint Paul, the most formidable of Christian advocates, sailed in to break a journey from Malta to North Africa. Syracuse fell from the centre of world events only in 831AD, when the Saracens shifted Sicily's capital north to Palermo.

BARELY ITALY AT ALL

Today, Ortygia is a strange but attractive mixture of narrow streets and wide sea- and sun-kissed promenades. Europe's wealthiest and most leisured classes parade here in their yachts, calling in from the south of France and Italy's prosperous North. Only occasionally does one come across the remnants of the Greek world: the Temple of Apollo, for instance which, in typical Italian style, shares the Largo XXV Luglio with a couple of low-key supermarkets and a gelateria. The palms and papyrus plants that shelter the temple are a reminder that one is closer to Tunisia than Turin. This is barely Italy at all, but the world of *magna graecia*, 'Greater Greece', with the flavours and sounds of the Arab world thrown in.

Unlike Palermo, on the other, northern side of Sicily, Syracuse was first wrecked and then strangely neglected by the Arabs, despite its obvious natural beauty and light, surrounded as it is on three sides by sea and sky. Where Ortygia merges with the modern city of Syracuse, there is a fish and fruit market where the casbah once stood.

The Arabs bequeathed a liking for sweet things when they left, and almonds in abundance. Early in the morning, computers stop for breakfast in true Syracuse style. Standing up in a ramshackle bar, they 'butter' almond granità on to a brioche, sipping strong coffee in between bites. With the temperature at 38°C (100°F), it makes sense. The soft, doughy brioche, neutral in taste, combines with the granità's sharp, crunchy shaved ice to create an almost unadulterated pleasure. I say 'almost' because care should be taken to eat it slowly: frozen nostrils ensue if this pleasure is rushed, or when a novice overloads the brioche.

The commuters head for their airconditioned buses. Those staying buy their groceries and head home. They won't emerge again into Syracuse's streets until four o'clock. Only the local ragazzi, jumping into Ortygia's rocky

harbour from the pedestal of its eastern promenade, brave the harsh sun. It was Cicero who said that Syracuse knew no day without sun. Or sugar.

One of the greatest paintings in the world resides in Syracuse: Caravaggio's *Burial of Saint Lucia*. Strikingly modern, framed with bodies clipped as if in a film, it's always watched over in the Galleria Regionale, by at least three attendants, who appear relatively unconcerned about the rest of the collection. Around the corner from the gallery, towards the seventh-century cathedral built on the ruins of the Greeks' Temple of Athene (a building whose foundations lay a further 1,200 years back), is the Antico Caffè Minerva. Glass-fronted with a terrace of tables facing the exposed brickwork of the duomo's oldest walls, its simple, stylish interior is cool. In the kitchen, it's cooler still. Tino di Bartolomeo, the owner, is a man who combines a cherubic profile and softy spoken demeanour with a burly, masculinity emphasised by enormous though delicate hands. His impression of a fallen angel wouldn't look out of place in a Caravaggio painting.

Opposite: Syracuse's Orecchio di Dionisio, 'Dionysius's ear', is a curved, artificial cavern, named by the great artist Caravaggio in 1608.

Left: Almond granità: the perfect antidote to the heat.

Sformato di carciofi
Artichoke timbale

Abundant in fruit, especially citrus, Sicily neglects its vegetables with a few exceptions: the artichoke, a distant relative of the thistle, is one. Like the Romans, who like to season artichokes with mint, Sicilians eat them raw or fry them in a little olive oil. This traditional Sicilian dish renders the vegetable more palatable to foreigners; the addition of Pecorino Sardo, the island's cheese made from sheep's milk, counteracts the artichoke's natural bitterness.

A LOT OF SUGAR DOES THE TRICK

Slightly shy, reticent and modest, Tino seems to find it odd that someone might be interested in his cool creations. Granità is really just a simple, sugary and uniquely refreshing frozen drink that's more popular than ice cream in the eastern quarter of Sicily – though they're no slackers when it comes to gelato either. Granità comes in many flavours: *gelso*, or mulberry is a Syracuse speciality, more flavourful than most styles; but *mandorla*, almond, is the classic, the flavouring subtle, even faint. In Palermo, the sweetener is syrup. In Syracuse it's lots of sugar that does the trick.

Granità is an easy pleasure that's hard work to make. Traditionalists like Tino rely on elbow grease to mix the almond paste and sugar in great metal bowls before adding it to the ice cream machines that find a welcome home in Sicilian kitchens, both professional and domestic. Their constant buzz and the reliance on airconditioning explain why power cuts are an all too common feature of the modern Sicilian summer; no lunchtime seems complete without a descent into darkness.

Opposite: Tino di Bartolomeo outside his Caffè Minerva. The sign lists the day's range of granità flavours.

The Sicilian diet is a healthy one, full of fresh fruit and the fish that dwell in the three seas – the Tyrrhenian, Mediterranean and Ionian – which surround the island. Sicilians drink less alcohol than other Italians, too: perhaps a legacy of their Arab past. That legacy is also apparent in the island's love of desserts. Granità and ice cream abound in Sicily, but strong competition for these exists elsewhere in Italy: the products of Naples are favoured by some, those of Calabria by others.

Ingredients

6 globe artichokes

½ medium onion, chopped

1 teaspoon freshly chopped
   flat-leaf parsley

1 tablespoon olive oil

1 egg, beaten

60g (2oz) grated Pecorino Sardo
   or Parmesan cheese

1. Remove the tough outer leaves of the artichokes, trim the spiky ends of the remaining leaves, cut off the stems and cut each artichoke into quarters.

2. Drop the artichoke into a large pan of boiling water, return to the boil and cook for 10 minutes. Drain and chop roughly.

3. Sauté the onion and parsley in the olive oil until the onion is golden.

4. Put the chopped artichoke and onion mixture into a bowl, add the egg and cheese, and mix well.

5. Place in a medium-sized oven tin and bake in a preheated oven at 200°C (400°F) gas mark 6 for 15 minutes.

Pasta alla Norma
Spaghetti with tomato sauce and aubergines

This is probably the most famous of all dishes named in honour of the heroine of the eponymous opera written by Vicenzo Bellini who was born in Sicily's 'second city', Catania.

Ingredients

2 medium aubergines

450g (1lb) ripe tomatoes

1 medium onion

100ml (3½ fl oz) olive oil

3 cloves garlic

handful chopped fresh basil

250g (10oz) spaghetti

100g (4oz) fresh ricotta

1. Slice the aubergines widthways into 5mm (½ in) slices and place them in salted water for 1 hour.

2. Roughly chop the tomatoes and the onion. Heat 2 tablespoons of olive oil in a saucepan and add the tomatoes, onion, whole garlic and chopped basil. Season with salt and pepper and cook gently for around 30 minutes, or until thick.

3. Strain the sauce through a sieve, pressing down in order to extract as much liquid as possible. Mix in 1 tablespoon of olive oil.

4. Dry the aubergines on kitchen paper and sauté slowly in the remaining oil.

5. Cook the spaghetti according to the instructions on the packet, drain, and cover with the tomato sauce. Sprinkle half the ricotta over it and stir well. Serve with the aubergine slices and the remaining ricotta on a different plate. Add to the spaghetti as necessary.

But there is one creation that, in its true state, is found only in Sicily, and is at its very best in Syracuse: cassata. It's a much abused name. Cassata means for many, even within Italy, a sometimes pleasant enough mixture of pistachio, strawberry and vanilla ice cream whose colours match the Italian flag. Most pizza chains in the world can dish one up. No Sicilian would recognise it.

Sicilian desserts were traditionally eaten on Catholic feast days and cassata is popular at Easter. It's even referred to as a 'sacrificial dish'. Outside Sicily, and sometimes within it, cassata is filled with ice cream. But the best cassatas are not, being variously rich concoctions of sponge cake, ricotta, and almond paste, topped with an outrageous array of candied fruit. Many now are mass-manufactured. Palatable certainly – standards slip only so far in Italy. But the real thing is handmade by artisans in Ortygia.

At first glance, the narrow streets of Ortygia bear a resemblance to those of Naples' *centro storico*. Its baroque alleys teem with locals dipping in and out of alimentari that sell the Italian staples of food and wine, along with the odd traditional barbershop, gelateria and tobacconist. But there's a prosperity, even a hint of chic to Ortygia that sets it apart from the rest of the island. The cafe is not the refuelling pit beloved of Neapolitans, but a place to pass the time, converse, even, God forbid, sit down without being charged for the privilege. It's also a place to eat, though the only course on offer is dessert.

A CLASSIC AFFAIR

Caffè Marciante is, I think, the classic Syracuse bar. It is close enough to the duomo and its piazza to pick up its fair share of the tourist trade, but not one to pander to it. It is a local cafe, despite its enviable location, and has remained largely unchanged since it was founded in the mid 1960s by Ernesto Marciante. Caffè Marciante bears all the hallmarks of a classic Italian bar of its vintage: a little

Above: Sharing refreshment in the Caffè Marciante.

Left: Coffee granità, which is common in the rest of Sicily – and most of southern Italy – takes second place to almond flavour in Syracuse

'This is the classic

Sicilian way. Well, there

are other ways too. But

this is my classic. It's

very exact. Takes time.

Bear with me.'

Giuseppe Marciante

neon, lots of zinc, functional chairs and tables and a constantly hissing Gaggia. Even the formidably bulky and unsmiling barman, fits the stereotype of the no-nonsense waiter as I ask the whereabouts of Ernesto's son, Giuseppe, the current owner. The barman leaves his bar for the backroom and returns followed by a darkly handsome Sicilian man in his 30s. Giuseppe Marciante, decked in his white chef's clothes, wipes his hand on his apron and shakes mine. 'Salve. Come through, this is where we make the cassata.'

I'd had a preview of Giuseppe's work as I'd ogled the contents of the tall, transparent, rectangular fridges that are spread throughout his cafe like Greek pillars. The cassata is sold divided into segments that ooze from their frilled little silver and paper trays. Unctuous might be the word for them. They look untamed, like wild sweets, as different to the tame, domesticated confections sold elsewhere as a dingo is to a dachshund. Would their taste be as rich and unbridled as their appearance?

A SICILIAN CLASSIC

Giuseppe's kitchen opens out onto the street. Passersby shout greetings and bits of local gossip to him as they pass. A great table – not unlike those of the pasta-makers of Bologna – dominates the space. Two boys, Alessandro and Francesco, attired too in white, hang on Giuseppe's every word. 'Fetch this, wash that, throw that out,' Giuseppe gently orders. He takes a long thin square of pane di spagna, 'Spanish bread', sponge cake in reality. He takes a small metal dish which he places upside down on the sponge to cut through it, leaving a perfect circle. He then cuts the circle into strips with which he lines the dish. It looks easy, but it isn't. There's an almost erotic delicacy to the way masters like Giuseppe Marciante and Tino di Bartolomeo perform their tasks, an almost unthinking, instinctive pursuit of perfection and satisfaction, a sense that there is no other way; that short cuts are out of the question.

A great dollop of ricotta cheese is spread by spatula over the sponge that has been moistened with a little sugar water. One of the boys passes Giuseppe some candied fruit and tiny chocolate drops that are dropped into the ricotta cheese. Another layer of sponge, cut and stripped in the same way as the first, is placed on top, moistened, and more ricotta is added. 'This is the classic Sicilian way,' Giuseppe assures me. 'Well, there are other ways too, but this is my classic. It's very exact. Takes time. Bear with me.'

Opposite:
Syracuse's baroque-fronted cathedral in the ancient square.

Left: Ice cream is ubiquitous and good throughout Sicily.

Below, left: Portions of cassata on display, sliced to revealing the dessert's many different layers.

Below: Almond sweets on sale in Caffè Marciante.

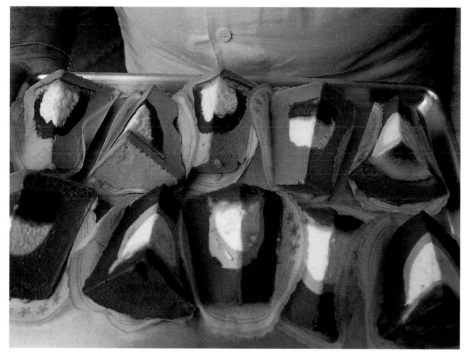

1. Giuseppe cuts sponge into slices.

2. A round baking tray cuts the sliced sponge to the correct shape.

3. The tray is lined with the strips of sponge.

4. Giuseppe adds ricotta and smooths it over the sponge.

5. Candied fruit and chocolate drops are added to the ricotta layer.

6. Further layers of sponge follow.

7. Next comes the almond and pistachio paste.

8. The cassata is turned out from the baking tray.

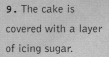

9. The cake is covered with a layer of icing sugar.

10. Giuseppe tops the cassata with an array of candied fruit and sweets.

Another box is brought from the fridge by one of the boys. It contains a glistening, sugary paste of almond and pistachio. Giuseppe softens it, rolls it out, and covers all the layers he's created so far in its smooth film, cutting the remainder from around the base.

Giuseppe takes a breather, and introduces me to his staff while Alessandro and Francesco create a rich paste of icing sugar in a pan over the stove. The mixture slips from

Giuseppe's wooden spoon onto the cake, to add another layer of almost obscene sweetness, which is again smoothed over the rest of the cake, enclosing it again. When it's perfect, Giuseppe raids a box of candied fruit, placing eight cherries at regular intervals around the edge of the cake. He cuts a fig – delicious and ubiquitous in Sicily – into eighths, and makes a display of that. Candied peel, quartered oranges, more figs are laid on top, as if in imitation of the baroque religious statuary found in every church on the island. This is a divine offering.

A SUGAR RUSH

The boys carry the finished cassata to a fridge where it will stay overnight before being divided into perfectly packaged parcels and displayed in the cafe's fridges. 'Here's one I made earlier,' Giuseppe says with a rare smile on his face. He hands me a portion. I'm almost fearful of the cassata, having seen what goes in it. Will it be cloying? A sugar rush? But, though sweet and rich, it's also surprisingly light, the sponge base balancing out the heavy paste. The barely candied fruit, still quite fresh, lends the cassata a 'natural' flavour missing from manufactured versions. 'Delicious,' I say. Giuseppe is pleased but surprised. 'It's what I do every day,' he says, with the nonchalance of a farmer for whom the splendours of nature are routine.

Watching both Tino and Giuseppe in action made me realise the often monotonous nature of their work and the near fanatical discipline it entails. Such skill and labour are experienced by us as a fleeting pleasure. But, bolstered by the close-knit community of Italian society and reinforced by the customers' appreciation, their task is made less arduous. Such a situation is typically Italian.

Above: Syracuse's master dessert-maker, Giuseppe Marciante, poses in front of the constantly changing window display of his family's cafe. Caffè Marciante has been in business since the 1960s.

Tonno all'agrodolce
Tuna in anchovy and caper sauce

It's hardly surprising that seafood should feature
prominently in the cuisine of an island surrounded by three
seas. Fresh tuna and anchovy abound in every Sicilian
market; capers are at their best in Salina, one of the
Aeolian islands off Sicily's north coast, and are also
plentiful on the fertile slopes of Mount Etna, Europe's
largest volcano, which dominates the east of the island.

Ingredients

2 tablespoons olive oil

3 cloves garlic, peeled and
  thinly sliced

3 fresh anchovy fillets

3 medium tomatoes, chopped

1 teaspoon capers

2 teaspoons fresh or 1 teaspoon
  dried marjoram

4 tuna steaks

1 tablespoon pesto sauce

1. Heat the olive oil in a
saucepan and sauté the
garlic for a few moments.
Add the anchovies and stir
until they have 'melted'.

2. Stir in the tomatoes and
reduce the mixture by
cooking it for 10 minutes
over a medium heat. Add the
capers and the marjoram, and
continue to reduce.

3. Meanwhile, cook the tuna
steaks under a medium grill.

4. Take the sauce off the heat,
add the pesto and stir.
Spoon a little over each
tuna steak and serve.

Granità alla mandorla

Almond granita

Granità comes into its own when the temperatures reach the high 30°Cs. Perfect with brioche and espresso, it's also a delicious dessert – though it won't be served this way in Sicily.

Ingredients

100g (4oz) caster sugar
600ml (1 pint) water
30g (1oz) almond paste

1. Stir the sugar and the water together in a saucepan over a low heat until all the sugar has melted.
2. Bring the sugar syrup to the boil over a high heat. Remove from the heat and blend in the almond paste
3. Pour the mixture into ice cube trays and freeze.
4. Just before serving, put the still-frozen ice cubes in a food processor and spin a couple of times to aerate the granita.
5. Serve in individual chilled ice cream dishes.

Cassata Siracusa

Cassata

There are probably as many ways to make cassata as there are sweet-makers in Sicily. However, this version comes close to capturing the flavours of the masterpieces Giuseppe Marciante creates daily.

Ingredients

350g (12oz) sponge cake

450g (1lb) ricotta cheese

125g (4 ½ oz) caster sugar

50g (2oz) small, dark chocolate drops

50g (2oz) candied fruit

180g (6oz) icing sugar

selection of candied fruits

1. Line a 21 x 13cm (8 x 5in) loaf tin with greaseproof paper. Thinly slice the sponge and evenly line the base and sides of the tin.

2. Mix the ricotta cheese and caster sugar in a blender and spoon it onto the sponge, then sprinkle the chocolate drops on top. Add the chopped candied fruit.

3. Melt the icing sugar in a bowl with a little water and spread about a third of it over the cassata. Cover the rest with a damp cloth, and leave it with the cassata overnight in the fridge.

4. Turn out the cassata, and cover the top with the remaining icing.

5. Decorate the top with candied fruits and chill in the fridge for at least 2 hours before serving.

INDEX

Headings and page numbers in
italic refer to recipes.

ACKNOWLEDGEMENTS

A book such as this is more dependent than most on the help and knowledge provided by others. It would not have been possible without the following: André Fucci of Lavazza, Turin. Ruggiero and Massimo Bovo and all at the Gatto Nero, Burano. In Bologna, the Salumeria da Bruno e Franco; Alessandra and Stefania Spisni; the University of Bologna library, and Bologna's tourist office. In Parma, Cristiana Clerici; Antonio Quelli; Latteria Social San Stefano; Consorzio del Prosciutto di Parma, and Salumeria Gardoni, Torrechiara. In Naples, Luigi Condurro and the staff of the Antica Pizzeria da Michele. The Di Gesù family of Altamura, in Puglia. Tino di Bartlomeo and Giuseppe Marciante in Syracuse, Sicily.

Tessa Boase and Nigel Richardson whose original commissions helped create this book. Greg Neale and Jonathan Gifford for their generous gift of time. Janet Ravenscroft and Paula Breslich at Breslich & Foss Ltd for their patience and skill; Anna Watson for even more patience; and to Elizabeth Healey for bringing these pages to life. Susan Murphy and Johnny Lay for yet more patience and good tastings. And last but not least, the Maionchi family of Lucca for their remarkable generosity and knowledge, especially Roberto Pelagi, 'The Boss', to whom this book is dedicated.